THAILAND

Text by Frena Bloomfield

Photographs by Derek M. Allan,
Dean Barrett and the
Tourism Authority of Thailand

A South China  Morning Post Publication

Published by the South China Morning Post
Publications Division, Tong Chong Street,
Quarry Bay, Hong Kong.

Set in Goudy Old Style type by Filmset Ltd.

Printed in Hong Kong by Yee Tin Tong Printing Press Ltd.

Acknowledgements
A big thank you to Louis Lulu Bull and Alan Goode who, besides being such good company, were a valuable source of additional information. The Tourism Authority of Thailand also gave help in planning itineraries.

Cover photo: *Wat Phra Doi Suthep, Chiang Mai*

ISBN 962 10 0028 9

Contents

Introduction
  History 7
  The People 9
  Religion 9
  Geography and Economy 11
General Information
  When to Go 12
  Climate 12
  Festivals 12
  Visas 15
  Customs 16
  Airport 17
  Tourist Information 17
  Health 18
  Money 18
  Tipping 18
  Transport 18
  Self-Drive 19
  Communications 19
  Media 20
  Shopping 20
  Do's and Don'ts 22
Food and Drink 25
Bangkok 32
  Transport 33
  Temples 38
  Other Places of Interest 45
  Nightlife 48
  Where to Eat in Bangkok 49
Around Bangkok
  The Ancient City 49
  Ayutthaya 53
Kanchanaburi and the River Kwai 56
  Nakhon Pathom 56
  Kanchanaburi 58
  River Kwai Resorts 60
The East Coast 62
  Pattaya 64
  Rayong 69
  Chanthaburi 70
  Trat 70

The Northeast 71
   Nakhon Ratchasima (Korat) 72
Chiang Mai and the North 76
   Handicrafts 82
   Markets 85
   Museums 87
   Eating Around Chiang Mai 87
   Trips out from Chiang Mai 89
The Hilltribes of Thailand 94
South of Chiang Mai
   Nan 104
   Lamphun 104
   Lampang 105
   Sukhothai 105
   Phitsanulok 108
The South 108
   Hua Hin 109
   Chaiya 112
   Surat Thani 113
   Ko Samui 113
   Nakhon Si Thammarat 118
   Songkhla 119
   Hat Yai 120
   Phuket 122
National Parks 126
Hotels in Bangkok 133
Index 138

Introduction

History

The Thai people originated in southern China, probably some 4,500 years ago. Over many centuries they steadily moved out of China and travelled further south and west until, by the 13th century, they had reached Burma and Laos. Pushing on further, they came into what is now Thailand and established their first capital at Sukhothai, which was at that time the northern capital of the declining Khmer empire.

It was the Sukhothai period which set the seal upon the real emergence of the Thai people under the leadership of King Ramkamhaeng. This king also helped to settle the states of northern Thailand and established friendly relations with the rulers of the surrounding countries, especially China.

From this period, too, date such things as the creation of a Thai alphabet and the establishment of a particular style of architecture now recognised as essentially Thai. Chinese craftsmen were brought in to set up the celadon pottery industry of Sawankhalok. King Ramkamhaeng became known as Rama the Great. He was so wise and merciful, it is said, that he had a bell hung at the entrance to his palace so that anyone in the kingdom who felt that he had been wronged could ring it and ask for royal intervention.

Indian Influences

Through trade with India and China the Thais began to make contact with Indian culture, resulting in its widespread absorption into Thai life. Thai classical dance, for example, owes much to classical Indian dance, and architecture has also been influenced. Most important of all perhaps was that Thailand absorbed the basic tenets of southern or Theravada Buddhism from Sri Lanka. This was the golden age of Sukhothai, and the influence of the Sukhothai kings extended south. But they were eventually eclipsed by a new dynasty led by King Ramathibodi, who set up his capital at Ayutthaya in 1350 AD.

Ayutthaya then more or less took over the role of Sukhothai by becoming the cultural, commercial and religious capital and entering a golden age of its own. Although now in ruins, there are still many signs of what it once was. During its heyday, it is said that the city had more residents than either Paris or London. It was built at the junction of three rivers with a canal completing what is effectively an island. Smaller canals linked many temples and palaces. In 1491 treaties were signed with various European countries, including France. In 1767 Ayutthaya fell for the second time to the Burmese and was ravaged, leaving it in ruins.

It took a great general to pull Thailand out of its servitude to the conquering Burmese warriors. General Phraya Tak Sin raised an army, took on the invaders in battle and drove them out of the country. The general ascended the throne as King Tak Sin. After a fifteen-year rule he was succeeded by another general, Chao Phya Maha Katsuksuk, who was the founder of the Chakri Dynasty.

Ties with the West

During the late 1800s, westernisation started influencing the Thai court in the sense that princes, courtiers and promising students were sent to study in Europe. Thanks to the diplomacy of King Rama IV, better known as King Mongkut, lasting relationships were established with Europe. This diplomatic initiative enabled Thailand, then known as Siam, to avoid the western colonisation that overtook all of its neighbours at this time. King Mongkut was followed by his son, King Chulalongkorn, who did much to modernise the country and bring education to the people. Gradual democratisation followed over the next few years in the reign of kings Rama VI and Rama VII, but even so a group of army officers staged a coup in 1932 and the absolute monarchy was downgraded to a constitutional one.

Thailand was on the side of the Allies during World War I, but in World War II the government was forced to sign a treaty of alliance with the Japanese. After the war, however, Thailand made peace with Britain while the US agreed not to acknowledge the Thai declaration of war. In 1946 Thailand joined the United Nations Organisation, the regional headquarters of which is in Bangkok.

Since that time Thailand has not had an uneventful history, though there has really been little to attract worldwide attention. Coups d'etat and revolutions have at times tumbled over each other in rapid succession. Fortunately the Thai monarchy has total support from all sectors of the population and has formed a constant and unchanging security against which the politics of army and state seem somehow altogether less important. Probably the worst single incident was the violent confrontation in 1973, during which a demonstrating crowd of 10,000 students demanded a return to democracy. In the slaughter which followed the government fell. In the years since then further upheavals and bloodshed have brought about more changes in government.

Thailand is in one of the most delicately balanced parts of the world, with communists to the north and east and capitalists to the south. Changes in the region have been profound in the last few decades, and it is perhaps not surprising that they have found their echo in Thailand itself. One thing that can be said, however, is that no foreigner should ever get involved in Thai politics.

Much of the country is extremely poor, and the main aim of the monarchy is that all Thais should have a right to the essentials of the good life—health, education and a chance to improve their lot. All the most important development projects in Thailand come under the royal banner. The strength of patriotism to be found among Thais often surprises outsiders. Thai students who go abroad to study cannot wait to get back to Thailand again. They seldom stay overseas, and the monarchy is regarded with genuine reverence and an awe which is impressive. It is hard to imagine that this little country, which really only identified itself in the 13th century, could ever allow its fierce independence to be jeopardised by any other considerations, whether political or economic. It is a country with a strong sense of tradition allied to great hopes for its own future.

The People

There are some 50 million Thais, about 85 percent of whom live in rural areas. At least 80 percent of the population are of Thai stock.

Before the arrival of the Thais from southern China, the land that is now Thailand was divided among a variety of different tribal and ethnic groups that had come to the country. People of Indian origin lived in Thailand around the 3rd century BC and left traces of their culture which are apparent even today. Before the Thais, the Mons and Khmers arrived together and set up separate civilisations. How much the Thais of today can be said to be totally separate from those earlier incursions is debatable.

There are a number of minority groups in Thailand today, the principle one being the Chinese—about three million of them. To say that is somewhat deceptive, however, since almost every Thai family has Chinese blood in it, but there is an odd ambivalence between the Thais and their feelings about the Chinese and their own blood inheritance. Many obviously Chinese-Thais describe themselves as Thai but add 'my father (or my mother) was Chinese'. In the southern provinces there are just over a million Malay-speaking Muslims, while 300,000 members of hilltribes live mainly in the North. More than 30,000 Vietnamese live in the Northeast, and the foreign population numbers about 13,000.

Religion

The official religion of Thailand is Buddhism, although it is the King's function to uphold the rights of all people to follow their religious beliefs. However, it is Buddhism which permeates the education, arts and official life of Thailand.

The Buddhism of Thailand is Theravada or southern Buddhism, the central belief of which is that all life is suffering, and that man can only be freed from the eternal cycle of rebirth by meditation and self-realisation.

The aim of such Buddhism is that each man tries to work out his own salvation.

Most Thai men become monks at some stage in their lives, sometimes for as little as a week, and the temple dominates life in most villages, if not quite so much in the cities. About four percent of the population is Muslim and less than 0.6 percent is Christian.

Geography and Economy

Thailand is about 500,000 square kilometres in size, approximately the area of France. From north to south it measures 1,650 kilometres and from east to west 800 kilometres.

It is found in the Indo-Chinese Peninsula, sharing borders with Burma to the west and north, Laos to the east and northeast, Kampuchea to the east and Malaysia to the south. It is a member of ASEAN, the Association of South East Asian Nations.

The topography is characterised by folded mountains, flat plains which flood during the rainy season, long low hills and a large number of beaches and lagoons.

The economy is based on agriculture, with rice as the most important export, followed by rubber, maize, tapioca, fresh prawns, tin, sugar and textiles. Each year Thailand exports almost three million metric tons of rice, earning more than 24 billion baht. Ten billion baht comes from tin and 15 billion from tapioca products.

Industrial investment is increasing in Thailand, with more firms producing construction materials, chemical products, garments, canned fruit and engine assembly. Other major industrial products include sugar, gunny sacks, cement, paper, vegetable oils, fertilisers and canned goods.

Thailand also ranks as one of the top ten fishing nations in the world, and about three percent of the gross national product comes from fishing. Shrimps are a leading marine export, earning nearly two billion baht a year. Timber production is extensive and Thailand exports teakwood all over the world.

An area of possible future development is natural gas. Preliminary investigation has revealed large reserves of natural gas beneath the sea surrounding the country. This has top priority from the government, as it is expected to prove to be an important foreign exchange earner in the future. The government is already involved in several joint venture deals with American oil companies.

General Information

When to Go

The high season for tourism is the three-month cool period from November to February when there are no floods and the temperature is ideal for visitors. Travelling is easier and quicker at this time too, and several of Thailand's major festivals occur during this period. However, it is reasonably pleasant the whole year round, so it should be a matter of individual choice.

Climate

Thailand has a tropical climate with high humidity and average temperatures of around 82°F. There are three seasons to the year: the hot season from March to June, the rainy season from July to October and the cool season from November to February.

The visitor must always beware of the burning rays of the sun, otherwise an unpleasant case of sunstroke may result. Apart from this precaution, only light summer clothing is necessary—natural fibres are coolest—and light shoes or sandals. An umbrella or plastic raincoat will be necessary in the rainy season and perhaps a sweater or light jacket for the cooler season.

Festivals

Most of the festivals of Thailand are religious in origin, either Buddhist or Brahminical, and are set according to the lunar calendar. Therefore they do not appear at the same time each year on the Gregorian calendar. For final dates on particular festivals, check with your travel agent or the nearest Thai consulate or embassy.

January: **New Year's Day** is celebrated throughout the country, starting with merit-making at the monasteries. Among younger people, it is much the same as New Year in the West, with gifts and cards being exchanged.

February (or early March): **Makha Puja** is the Buddhist All Saints' Day during which merit-making ceremonies are performed to mark the four great events of the Lord Buddha's lifetime. On the full moon, 1,250 Arahats came simultaneously, but without prior arrangement, to pay homage to the Buddha. On the evening of the same day, the Buddha delivered a discourse known as the *Ovadha Patimokha*.

April: The **Songkran** festival falls on April 13 and is the traditional Thai New Year. This is when the farmers have completed the harvest and have some time to spare for enjoyment and religious affairs. The festival includes merit-making, popular entertainment and the traditional skittles game called *saba*. There is also a lot of water-throwing, and

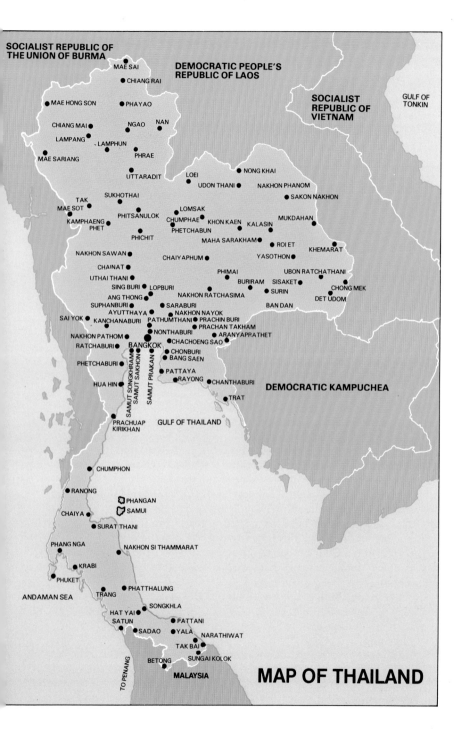

MAP OF THAILAND

visitors are not spared, so wear your oldest clothes that day or suffer! People set fish free to make merit and hold memorial services dedicated to their departed ancestors.

May: **Visakha Puja** falls on the full moon of May and marks the birth, enlightenment and passing into nirvana of the Buddha. This is a great Buddhist holy day. People flock to the temples for a day of religious ceremonies, and many candlelight processions are held.

May: The **Ploughing Ceremony** is a great state occasion, dating back to the time of the Sukhothai period. It marks the start of the planting season and the King himself usually presides over the festival. It was a farming ritual originally.

July: The period of **Khao Pansa,** or Buddhist Lent, starts on the first day of the waning moon of the eighth lunar month (usually in July). The celebration is for monks who will be confined to their monastery for the three rainy months. Every year it is marked by a ceremony in the Chapel Royal. It is a popular festival in which people go to the temples and make offerings to the monks. Lent itself continues until September.

August: The **Queen's Birthday** falls on August 12th and is an official holiday.

September: **Kin Kuai Salak** is a traditional northern Thai festival falling in September. The name translates literally as 'the partaking of food in a basket obtained in a draw', and it is quite an involved procedure. On the eve of the festival townspeople—especially young girls—pack dry food such as uncooked rice, salt, chilis, onions and other things in a wicker basket, while old people decorate raised trays with puffed rice, incense, candles and flowers. Each girl tucks in a note naming herself and the people to whom the merit is dedicated. On the actual festival day there is a procession to the temple, and after a religious ceremony the baskets are taken and the names of all concerned are read aloud.

October: **Ching Pret** is the Thai version of the Chinese Hungry Ghosts festival in which the spirits from hell—or *pret,* as they are called—are allowed to wander the earth for fifteen days from the first day of the waning moon in the 10th lunar month. Food and offerings are made and people make merit on behalf of their dead. After the ceremony is over, people scramble for the food which is believed to bring good health and merit.

October: **King Chulalongkorn Memorial Day** falls on October 23 and is observed as a tribute to the king who died in 1910. Ceremonies are held at the king's statue near Parliament House, and many people bring offerings.

Mid-October/mid-November: **Kathin** takes place after Lent, so the date varies from mid-October to mid-November. It is the time when new robes are presented to the monks by laymen in gratitude for the monks' good example in practising and teaching the word of the Buddha.

The popular Loy Krathong festival

Usually the King leads the people in this ceremony. In years past he led a procession of barges along the river to Wat Arun, the Temple of Dawn, in magnificent pageantry.

November: The **Loy Krathong** festival is probably the most popular of the year among Thais and foreigners, and certainly one of the most beautiful. Said to have originated in the Sukhothai period, it consists of setting candles afloat on tiny rafts of leaves and flowers. It is supposed to symbolise the shedding of sin, as well as being a thanksgiving to the gods of the water. It marks the end of the rainy season, and is a very joyful occasion.

December: The **King's Birthday** and **National Day** falls on December 5th and is celebrated with official and religious rituals.

December: **Constitution Day** commemorates the signing of the first constitution on December 10th, 1932.

Visas

Nationals of most countries who land in Thailand are allowed to stay for 15 days if they hold onward confirmed tickets, but read on for details.

Those arriving from Malaysia by boat, train or motor vehicle can stay 15 days without a visa if they hold onward tickets. Passengers holding valid passports are admitted with the following visas: Transit, up to 30 days;

A colourful religious procession

Tourist, up to 60 days; Non-Immigrant, Diplomatic, Official and Special, up to 90 days.

Citizens of ASEAN countries with valid passports but no visas can stay up to 15 days.

Hong Kong British passport holders can stay for 15 days without a visa provided they hold confirmed onward tickets.

Citizens of the Republic of Korea with valid passports are admitted for 90 days.

Where people would like to stay for more than 15 days but have no Thai consulate or embassy access, they should write direct to the Immigration Division, Soi Suanplu, Bangkok 10120, Thailand.

Customs

You may not bring into Thailand illegal narcotic drugs, obscene literature or firearms without a permit. You are allowed to bring in any reasonable amount of clothing, toilet articles and professional instruments duty free. The same applies to used household articles.

You are allowed one still camera and one cine camera without paying duty. Five rolls of still film or three of movie camera film are duty free.

You may bring in cigarettes, cigars or smoking tobacco not exceeding 250 grammes in weight or not more than 200 cigarettes. One litre each of wine or spirits are allowed in duty free.

Some plants, fruits and vegetables are banned. To find out which, you must contact the Department of Agriculture, Bangkok, Tel: 5790151. To bring in animals, permission of entry can be obtained at the airport and vaccination certificates are required. If the animal is coming by sea, application must be made at the Department of Livestock, Bangkok, Tel: 2817599.

You are allowed to bring in only 500 baht in Thai currency, and you must declare any amount of foreign currency above US$2,000.

Airport

You will have to go through immigration first, followed by a desultory customs check.

You will probably be mobbed by taxi drivers crowding outside the arrival lounge. If you are new to Bangkok, it is less hassle to take the airport limousine to your hotel at 280 baht. It is not actually a limousine at all, but a 12-seat minibus, and the service is slow mainly due to Bangkok's horrendous traffic. You can get a taxi cheaper—anything from 80 up to 200 baht according to your bargaining powers and the number of taxis waiting. There are a lot of private pirate cabs, and they are reasonably honest on the whole once you have negotiated the fare. As very few ordinary Thais can read English well, or for that matter understand your spoken English, it would be a very good idea to get your destination written down by someone at the information desk before you leave the airport.

Tourist Information

The Tourism Authority of Thailand has its main office in Bangkok at Ratchadamnoen Avenue. They have a lot of good information there but for some reason it is quite hard to get it out of them. You will have to insist nicely on getting a complete range of brochures, and they also have a number of cyclostyled pages of information on different destinations. They are even *more* reluctant to give you these, but if you are determined you may get them. The office is very untidy and cluttered, so perhaps their reluctance is merely because they cannot actually find most of the stuff.

There are TAT offices in other major cities of Thailand and in all important tourist destinations. Your first visit in any city should be to the TAT local office to collect maps, help and information. The Chiang Mai office is notable, in a land full of agreeable friendly people, for its sulky girls, but the Pattaya office has splendidly helpful, pleasant staff.

One note: TAT people mainly think in terms of you buying package tours and commercial trips, so do not take their discouragement of your own plans for adventure too seriously.

Health

There are no specific health requirements for entering Thailand unless you have come from a cholera-infested area.

Thailand, or at least Bangkok, is a good place to get sick. It has some of the best medical facilities anywhere in Asia, and good enough to beat those of quite a number of places in Europe. There are numerous private hospitals and clinics in Bangkok of excellent standards. If you get sick, you could try Bangkok Christian Hospital, 124 Silom Road, Tel: 2336981, or the Seventh Day Adventist Hospital at 430 Phitsanulok Road.

Follow the usual precautions of any tropical country—drink hot drinks or sealed cold drinks if you are not sure whether the water has been boiled or not. Resist ice in your drinks and avoid salads. Even if you fail to do all this, you are not in much danger of anything. If you do get diarrhoea, stop travelling, stop eating and drink as much as you can until the attack is over. Do not take medicines which merely paralyse the bowel as this does not address the real problem. If the diarrhoea persists badly beyond a couple of days, consult a doctor.

There is malaria in Thailand, so you should be taking anti-malaria tablets. To keep away hungry mosquitoes you need a mosquito net, a coil or some good repellent. Get these in Bangkok.

Money

The Thai baht is tied to the US dollar. There are 100 satang in each baht. Coins come in denominations of 25 satang, 50 satang, one baht and five baht, and everything else is in notes. As they are all clearly marked and of different colours, you should have no problems. Do not carry notes of too large denomination upcountry, as people there may not be able to change them. Traveller's cheques could also cause problems in the provinces. Make sure you have enough to budget on while you are travelling.

There is no black market currency racket in Thailand, and the exchange rate is always around 23 baht to one US dollar, with slight fluctuations.

Tipping

Many people, especially in less grand places, do not expect tips and even two baht can delight them. In more commercial settings about ten percent will do, if there is no service charge on the bill.

Government tax on food, drink and hotel bills can easily bump the bill up by about 15 percent.

Transport

There are excellent train and bus services throughout Thailand. Because buses are cheaper, and quite often quicker, most people prefer them, but the chances of highway robbery are greater on a bus. The more expensive the bus, the more it could be a robber's target, but do not lose sleep over this remote possibility.

Every major city has a bus terminal, and it is usually not even necessary to book ahead. You can just go in and buy your ticket. Fares are fixed and you will not be cheated. For trains, it can be a hassle to go to the station to buy ahead, which can be necessary on some of the more popular routes such as the overnight express from Bangkok to Chiang Mai. This is one instance where it may well be worth paying a travel agent the commission to do it for you. Otherwise, in Bangkok, you must go to the station appropriate to your destination not more than ten days ahead and buy. For the North, Northeast and most express trains to the South, go to Hualampong Station on Rama IV Road, for the East go to Makkasan Station on Makkasan Road and for slow trains to the South go to Thonburi Station.

There are three classes, and first and second classes have sleepers. For long overnight journeys this is a good idea, but for daytime journeys even third class is pleasant. It can also be a lot more interesting. On all trains make sure your luggage is safely near you and, when you sleep, hug it like your long-lost child.

Food is available on all trains and it is certainly edible. You cannot expect much more. The best food is in third class because vendors board the trains and peddle it from station to station.

Train timetables are available at TAT offices and, of course, at the railway stations.

Self-Drive

You can hire cars, starting somewhere around 800 baht a day plus. Unless you know Thailand, it would not be a good idea to drive. Thai drivers are pretty erratic, to put it mildly, and big vehicles hurtle along the highways with very little regard for any other road user. All the usual international names in car-hire are in Bangkok. Look them up in the English-language Yellow Pages.

Communications

The Post and Telegraph Department on New Road is open from 7.30am to 4.30pm Mondays to Fridays and from 9am to noon on Saturdays, Sundays and holidays. Letters and phone calls should go from here, as it is quick. Calls from your hotel are likely to take literally hours to get through. If your letters are important, send them registered. Postcards tend not to arrive at their destination safely in 50 percent of cases.

You can use this post office as a poste restante for your own mail.

Media

There are two excellent daily newspapers which come out every morning, the *Bangkok Post* and the *Nation*. The afternoon *Bangkok World* is another daily, as is the *Herald Tribune*.

There are four television channels, virtually all in Thai, although you can catch a twice-daily newscast in English, but on the whole unless you speak Thai you will have to do without television.

Shopping

Thailand is especially rich in handicrafts, and you can find some very attractive things at modest prices.

Among the things you should look into are:

Thai Silk—Available everywhere in various qualities and at all kinds of prices. Whether you go to Jim Thompson's for top of the market silk or to a local market to buy lengths of rough country style silk, it will still be a bargain compared to what you pay overseas. Compare prices and bargain hard.

Tailoring—You can get good, cheap and fast tailoring done in Bangkok. You can get things made in 24 hours and even the best-fitted suit need take no more than three days. Thailand is not Savile Row, however. A man's suit of imported fabric could be around 2,500 to 4,000 baht; of local fabric from 1,800 to 2,400 baht. A woman's full-length Thai silk gown could be around 1,500 baht and a dress 900 baht.

Gemstones and Jewellery—Be careful unless you really know your stones. Find out a reasonable market price per carat for jewellery and know that if you are being offered something much cheaper, it can't be good. Gold is often wrongly marked and dishonestly sold in Thailand, so the same warning applies. Do not listen to touts or tour bus operators. Take risks on small inexpensive pieces, but on the best be sure. Get a detailed receipt for any item that you buy, including the quality of gold, the gemstone and its weight. If it is really a big buy, ask the jeweller to go with you to an independent assayer or at least have the receipt marked 'subject to identification and appraisal by a registered gemologist'. No honest jeweller would refuse this.

The stones found in Thailand's gem stores are rubies from Thailand, Burma, Kampuchea and Sri Lanka, Thai black star sapphires and green sapphires, and garnets from Africa and South America. Emeralds from Pakistan, India and South America are available. Good buys are the South American topaz and the Australian opal, due to lower cutting costs in Thailand.

Nielloware—This black and silver jewellery is actually made by decorating metal with inlaid designs filled with a mixture of sulphur and silver, copper or lead. The Thais call it *thom,* and it is said to have been

Dolls are a popular handicraft item

discovered during the golden age of Ayutthaya. You can get niello jewellery, cigarette cases, lighters and ashtrays.

Bronzeware—Bangkok is one of the few places in the world where articles in bronze are still being made. You can get a complete range of table utensils, bells and all kinds of other artefacts.

Pottery—The centre for this is Chiang Mai, and the pottery is made of soft earthy colours with delicate greens and other natural glazes. You can buy vases big and small, bowls, plates, ashtrays, lamps and even complete sets of tableware.

Wood-carving—Another Chiang Mai-based art, usually using teakwood. Small carved objects like bowls, salad servers, candlesticks and musical instruments can be found.

Wickerwork—Throughout the whole of Thailand, in many little villages scattered all over the countryside, villagers make artefacts from rattan, bamboo, palm-leaf, sisal and banana straw. Look for baskets, furniture, handbags, slippers, among other things.

Do's and Don'ts

Fortunately, the Thais are themselves so courteous that they are likely to overlook the worst of what you might do, but there are a few necessary politenesses you should be aware of.

Heads are considered sacred and therefore you should never touch another person's. This also applies to children, so you should resist the temptation to pat little children on the head or pinch their chubby little cheeks.

Feet, on the other hand, are considered quite unacceptable. Therefore you must ensure that yours do not point at anyone. You might think this unlikely, but once you become aware of what your feet are doing it is surprising how often you catch them at it. Don't sit with one leg crossed on top of your other leg, because the sole of your foot will certainly be pointing at someone then. When talking to a Thai, don't stick your legs straight out in front of you so your feet point at him or her—this is also very rude. Never indicate anything with your feet.

Hands. Although not as bad as your feet, your left hand is not considered clean—because it is assumed that you wash yourself with it after defecation. So do not touch people with it and do not hand anything to others with your left hand. Keep it off the table when eating. Do not point at things with your left hand, and never at people.

Height. Thais, you will notice, always try to keep their heads lower than their elders or those worthy of respect. It is somewhat impractical now to be as strict about this as they once were but the general principle still exists. A token effort at not standing over others is acceptable, so bend your body somewhat when, for example, you have to pass between others.

Religion. Buddhism is, of course, the main religion of Thailand, although there is a significant minority of Muslims. Great respect must be shown in all dealings with Buddhism. You must never clamber upon Buddhist statues to get better pictures or for any other reason. You must never treat even the tiniest Buddha image with disrespect. In temples, or 'wats' as they are usually called, you must remove your shoes before entering the inner shrine, and your dress should be what you would consider decent for a semi-formal occasion—so no shorts for men or women, certainly no beach clothing, and decorous behaviour is the order of the day.

Monks are treated with great respect in Thailand. They even get 50 percent discounts on Thai Airways, which is a charming gesture. If you are a woman, you must never sit next to a monk or touch him in any way at all. If you do, the poor man will have to undertake elaborate purification rituals.

It is no good having your own feminist ambitions to change any of this. You can't, and outside your own culture you don't have the right to try, so please observe this taboo. If you want to give something to a monk and you are female, you must first either hand it to a secular male or place it on a cloth which the monk will set down before him.

Royalty. However much they may change governments, the Thais are unfailingly loyal to their Royal Family. They feel great devotion to the

monarchy, and while they may not expect you to feel the same, they will certainly expect you to behave with the utmost propriety towards anything to do with the King and Queen of Thailand. Thus, in cinemas, when the King's picture is shown and the royal anthem played, you must stand immediately and stay stockstill until it is finished. No shuffling and no moving.

No image of the King must ever be insulted, so be careful you don't do it. Don't forget that the King's image is also on postage stamps, so make sure you stick them on properly. Never make insulting remarks about the Thai Royal Family.

Smiling. The Thais do a great deal of this, and it is as well to realise what a complex thing a smile may be in Thailand.

It may and often does denote pleasure and friendliness, as in most Western countries. However, it is also the social tool for all situations—for apology, embarrassment, to express sorrow, to cover anger, so if you are caught in a difficult situation and everyone is smiling, don't assume they don't take it seriously.

When it comes to yourself, you are also supposed to keep smiling no matter what. It is considered very low-class to lose your temper, so the counsel of perfection is that you keep smiling grimly until the situation is sorted out.

Food and Drink

The timid eater will find an approximation of Western food in most parts of Thailand, but the resemblance gets fainter the further you get from the city centres. In fact Thai food itself is splendid stuff, and it would be a pity if you allowed those scare stories of fiery tongue-destroying dishes to stop you trying. That said, it must be admitted that many Thai dishes are very hot, but you can always ask for them to be made milder for you.

Apart from the excellent cooked dishes, there is also a wonderful selection of fresh fruit available virtually all over the country. It must be the best range of tropical fruit anywhere in Asia. The best place to buy is obviously in the market, where you will undoubtedly be overcharged. However, just think about what such exotica would cost you at home, and pay up with a smile.

As English is not widely spoken in Thailand, particularly outside Bangkok and Chiang Mai, an approximate pronunciation guide has been added. Your attempts will cause great gales of laughter, of course, or at best stifled giggles, but try anyway. Also, point—but only with your right hand —at what you would like to eat.

There are many open-air food stalls in Thailand, and there is no real need to be afraid of the food cooked there. Thailand, after all, is not India, and travellers do not usually fall prey to the perils of dysentery as they do

on the sub-continent. Nevertheless, it would be a good idea to stick with boiled water if you can, or bottled water or bottled drinks and hot drinks. Of course you should not add ice to those cold drinks, as it will almost certainly not be made from boiled water. Many people ignore all these precautions in Thailand without coming to any harm.

It is wise not to eat raw vegetables, however, as you may get worms.

Drinks

Nam plao	water
Nam khaeng plao	crushed ice
Cha yen	iced tea with milk
Cha dam yen	iced black tea with sugar
Cha dam ron	hot black tea with sugar
Cha ron	hot tea with milk
Kafae ron	hot coffee with milk
Kafae dam	hot black coffee with sugar
Kafae dam mai sai namtan	hot black coffee without sugar
Kafae yen	iced coffee with milk
O liang	iced black coffee with sugar
Owanteen	Ovaltine
Ko ko	cocoa
Nom	milk

Breakfast

Khanom pang ping	toast
Nnoei	butter
Yem	jam
Khai luak	soft-boiled egg
Khai tom	hard-boiled egg
Khai dao	fried egg
Khai chiao/khai fu/khai tot	plain omelette

Curry Dishes

Gaeng massaman	rich beef curry with peanuts (not hot)
Gaeng ka ri	mild Indian-style curry, usually with chicken and potatoes
Gaeng gai	spiced chicken stew
Gaeng nua	spiced meat stew
Gaeng pla duk	spiced catfish stew
Gaeng som	fish and vegetable stew

Fried Dishes

Khao phat	fried rice
Priao wan	sweet and sour pork with vegetables
Phak bung phat	morning glory
Hae kung	thin slices of shrimp cracker eaten with a side order of Chinese syrup
Mi krob	crisp thin noodles with tiny scraps of meat, shrimp, egg and sweet and sour sauce
Po pia	spring roll (beansprouts, pork, crabmeat)
Po pia tot	spring roll (same but fried)
Nua phat namman hoi	fried beef with green onion in oyster sauce
Dok kalam phat mu, kung, gai, nua	fried pork, shrimp, chicken or beef with cauliflower

Soups

Gaeng chut	mild soup with vegetables, shrimp, chicken and pork
Gaeng liang	Thai vegetable soup
Tom yam	chili hot and sour soup with either pork, shrimp, beef, chicken or fish.
Khao tom mu	mild rice soup with pork
Khao tom pla	mild rice soup with fish
Khao tom kung	mild rice soup with shrimp
Tom khlong	salted fish boiled with tamarind and onions

Egg Dishes

Khai tot sai mu	pork omelette
Khai yat sai	omelette with meat, onion and pea stuffing

Rice and Meat Dishes

Khao man gai	sliced chicken and rice with chicken gravy
Khao na pet	sliced roast duck and rice
Khao na gai	sliced chicken with bamboo shoots, spring onions and gravy on rice
Khao mu daeng	sliced cooked pork with egg and gravy on rice
Khao mu tot	sliced fried pork on rice
Khao lat na nua	fried vegetables and meat in gravy on rice

Noodles

Kuai tiao lat na	flat white noodles with meat and vegetables

Kuai tiao haeng	white noodles with shredded meat and vegetables
Kuai tiao nam	same, with broth
Kuai tiao phat thai	thin white noodles, with beansprouts and other ingredients, but no meat
Ba mi nam	egg noodles, meat and broth
Ba mi haeng	same, no broth
Ba mi na mu	fried egg noodles with pork
Ba mi na phak	same, with vegetables
Ba mi krob lat na kung	crisp fried egg noodles with shrimps
Ba mi krob lat na mu	same, but pork
Ba mi krob lat na gai	same, but chicken
Kieo nam	wonton soup
Kieo haeng	wonton with vegetables and spices

Fish Dishes

Pla priao wan	sweet and sour fried fish
Kam pu tot	fried crab claws
Kam pu nung	steamed crab claws
Hu cha lam sai pu	shark's fin soup with crabmeat
Gung tot krob	crisp fried prawns
Pla tot	fried fish
Pla nam khao	stewed pomfret

Thai Puddings

Sang kha ya	custard
Sang kha ya kha nun	jackfruit custard
Ma phrao sang kha ya	coconut custard
Thong yib	sweet egg-petals
Thong yot	sweet egg-drops
Foi thong	sweet egg-shred
Khanom mo kaeng	egg sweet plate
Lot chong nam ka thi	rice drops in sweet coconut sauce
Kluai buat chi	banana in sweet and salty coconut cream
Luk tan chuam	palm seeds cooked in syrup
Wan waan	sweet jelly
Wan nam chuam	jellied syrup
Ta ko	gelatin top with coconut cream
Khao niao kaeo	glutinous rice cooked in coconut cream and sugar

When trying to pronounce any of the above, remember that TH and PH are pronounced as a breathy T and P. There are a lot of aspirates in Thai, and the H merely shows this is one of them. There are also tones, which I have not attempted to show, since Thais are usually able to work out what you really mean, even if you say it wrongly. They will, of course, laugh at your attempts, but it is very friendly laughter, so try not to worry.

Food prices are usually modest. In cheap eating places and at food stalls, the custom is to order, eat and pay. There are no menus as such. This can result in overcharging of visitors, usually on the assumption that they can afford it.

If this bothers you, check out the price *before* you order as it will be more of a problem to argue the issue after you have eaten. In regular restaurants there are menus, often in both Thai and English.

Alcohol

Alcohol is freely available throughout Thailand. Imported drinks are expensive, as you might expect, but Thailand does make a lot of its own. Perhaps the most famous is the deadly but deceptive Mekhong whisky. This amber-coloured killer slips down very easily and can cause an enormous headache and hangover afterwards. Real Thai enthusiasts love it, so do try, but don't say you weren't warned.

There are also various very local brews made from fermented coconut and such. Try them if you must.

There are some good lager beers being made in Thailand. The big three are Singha, Amarit and a new one called Kloster. Everyone has his favourite and mine is Singha, but taste and decide for yourself. Beer also is fairly expensive compared with food. You may well find, if you eat cheaply, the drink costing more than the food.

Coffee

Coffee is pretty so-so around Thailand. It tends either to be the powdered stuff, or a brew made from tamarind which is rather bitter and ersatz in taste.

Fruits

Banana—There are many varieties of these all over Thailand, and they are plentiful and cheap.

Custard apple—This curious creature is rather like a round green hand grenade which you break in half and then eat the delicious little juicy segments nestling inside.

Durian—Much controversy surrounds this giant green legless hedgehog of a fruit. It has an oddly fetid smell and is therefore banned from hotels and aircraft, but its taste is excellent—if you like it. Try it once at least.

Guava—A pear-shaped tooth-breaker with sweet flesh full of tiny seeds.

Jackfruit—Cousin to the durian but less controversial. This is often

Thailand is a fruit lovers' paradise

used in cooking, but the seeds inside are covered by sweet yellow flesh which is good to eat raw.

Longan—This looks a very boring, small, dull brownish yellow, round fruit, but inside lurks a wonderful treat—soft, sweet, fleshy fruit rather like lychee in taste.

Mango—The wonderful mango needs no introduction.

Mangosteen—This is a dark purple fruit, round and about the size of a large plum, with sweet fleshy segments inside. Just break open the rough purple skin for interior delights, but do not try to eat the seeds.

Orange—There are many varieties of orange in Thailand, some of them green but ripe.

Papaya—Also known as the pawpaw, this is a long marrowish looking fruit, green or orange outside with orange flesh within. It is good for breakfast, and is said to be an aid to good digestion and able to settle an uneasy stomach.

Pineapple—Lots of these too, and very inexpensive. Street traders sell them already sliced and dipped in salt, which makes a delicious and refreshing snack.

Pomelo—Pomelo are big coarse cousins to the grapefruit, but sweeter.

Rambutan—Like a red hairy lychee with soft sweet flesh inside.

Watermelon—No need to buy a whole one, just get slices.

Northern Thai Food

When visiting northern Thailand you should try some of the regional dishes, as they are somewhat different from the usual run of Thai food, and also often use sticky rice instead of ordinary steamed rice. Some people think sticky rice is an acquired taste, but I think it is delicious.

Khao niao is the name for sticky rice. You are supposed to take a little ball of it and eat it with your fingers, together with whatever is the main ingredient of your meal.

Roast chicken done the northern Thai way (which is actually the Laotian way) is also eaten with the fingers. The chicken is deliciously tender and chopped into finger-sized pieces.

Sai ooua is Chiang Mai sausage; small, fatty and spicy.

Larp is actually from the Northeast, but it is also popular in northern Thailand, especially since it goes well with sticky rice. It is made from beef, liver, pork and duck (any or all of these) ground up with vegetables and spices. It is served up with fresh vegetables—cabbage, mint leaves, green beans and cucumbers. It can be very hot, so best to indicate you want it less so by saying *Mai aow phet-phet na.*

Sticky rice is also served as a dessert. You can eat it topped with coconut cream, various condiments, fruits and *toa dam,* or black beans.

Khao niao dam is translated as black sticky rice, but it is actually a brownish-red colour and delicious to eat.

Bangkok

The 'City of Angels' has an extraordinary personality of its own which somehow manages to overcome disadvantages which would be enough to destroy any other city as a tourist centre. It is undeniably dirty, fume-laden, noisy, often flooded for weeks on end with greasy water, full of vice and prostitution—and yet, and yet. Its charm is that it is still very Thai—warm, friendly and kind of fun.

There is no way of avoiding the fact that Bangkok is something of a disaster area as a capital. It has suffered from all the worst things that can happen to a city. Earlier this century it was apparently a gracious city of boulevards, canals and trees. Well, the trees were cut down and the canals filled in, so there is no shade in the tropical humid streets any more, and nowhere for the water to go when it rains. Modern concrete buildings everywhere have replaced the stylish and useful Thai wooden houses which were naturally cool.

However, the temples still dominate the skyline with their startlingly golden pointed roofs, and Thais themselves have a pride in their country, King and future. Somehow this helps to make the basically agreeable atmosphere for which Bangkok is famous. There is no anti-foreign feeling as can be found in many Asian cities these days, and the visitor is always made welcome and shown great courtesy.

One confusing thing about Bangkok is that when you are trying to get your bearings, there seems to be no real city centre. There are instead various areas identified by their main feature or their centre of interest. There is one area where the most important government and United Nations buildings are found, around Ratchadamnoen Avenue. There is Chinatown. There is the banking area of Silom Road. There is the Royal Palace and other royal buildings. There is the nightlife area around Patpong, and so on.

So the first key to Bangkok is to decide how you are going to get around it from one area to another, since this is a big sprawling urban puddle of a city. If you only plan to take a few guided tours, there is no need to worry, but if you would like to do better than that and begin to get the measure of this rich and amiable city, you can.

Transport

Taxis—These creatures are without fare meters (when they had them they never used them). But that isn't a problem. Just check with your hotel or a Thai friend and find out what the fare should be and offer this to the driver. After a day or so, you'll be so used to it that even taxi drivers will be convinced. Most fares are between 20 and 50 baht, and you pay not so much by the distance as by the time of the day. In the rush hours, morning and night, you can easily pay double for the time spent in traffic jams—and fair enough too.

Samlors—These are the three-wheeled scooter taxis universally known as 'tuktuks'. Bargain again and expect a five to 10 baht reduction on the taxi fare. At night avoid them, as robberies have been reported via these vehicles. When in them, hold your bag and valuables close in case a motorcycle thief whizzes by.

Buses—These really are a pretty good, cheap and efficient way to get around Bangkok. Buy the city bus and road map, cheaper from the TAT than elsewhere, and start travelling. Aircon bus fares range from five to 15 baht. Non-aircon are less.

Boats—Those expensive tours are not entirely necessary. Go down to the Tha Phra Chan area, next to Thammasat University, and ride the river taxi for a few baht as far as it goes past the fascinating houses on stilts and the whole absorbing world of the water's edge.

There are many things to see in and around Bangkok, and you don't have to take an arranged tour. With your bus map, or at least a fair idea of what taxi fares should be, you can cover a lot of the city yourself. It is a very safe city, by the way, but don't invite trouble by flashing your gold and being careless with your wallet or purse.

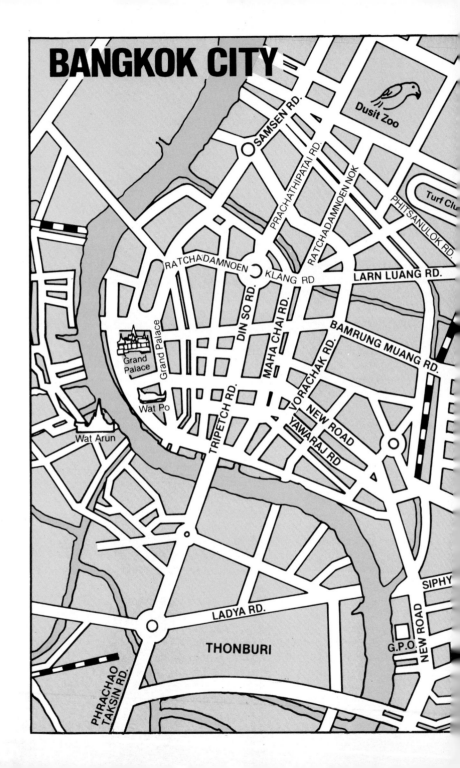

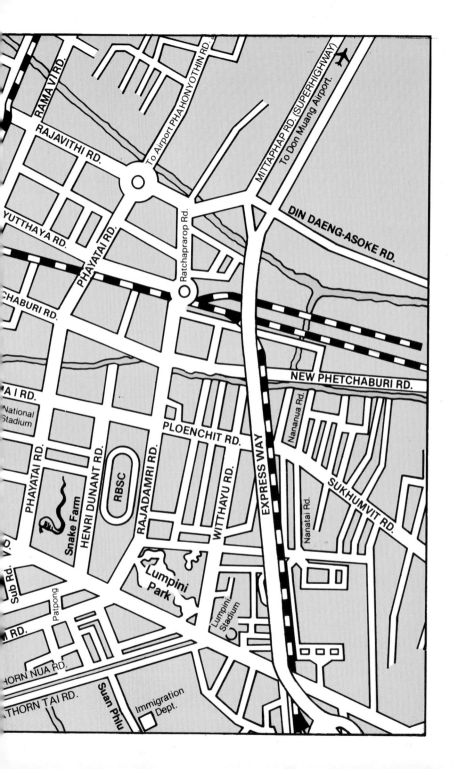

The samlor—cheap and convenient urban transport

What to See Around Bangkok

Temples

Temples are one thing Thailand is not short of, and Bangkok has some of the most stunning of all. Even if you think you don't want to see a temple, go anyway. They are such a richly exotic experience, and Thai temples are so completely different from any other Asian temples that you would be foolish to overlook them.

Start with the **Wat Phra Kaeo** and the **Grand Palace.** Both these buildings are contained in one huge compound on Na Phra Lan Road near the Pramane Ground. They are surrounded by tall white walls and occupy one-square mile. They are stunning—rich, jewelled, tiled in splendid glazed and gilded tiles, and the temple itself has the fly-away roof eaves so characteristic of Thai temples.

The palace was built in 1782 and has been added to ever since, so it represents a fair mixing of architectural styles. Room after splendid room follows on throughout the several groups of buildings, and it will give you some idea of the magnificence with which Thai royalty has been surrounded. It is used only on rare ceremonial occasions now, as the actual royal residence is elsewhere.

A giant sentinel stands guard over Wat Po

The Wat Phra Kaeo is better known as the Temple of the Emerald Buddha. It shelters the most sacred image in the kingdom of Thailand, one which is thought to give occult power to the King's reign. This talisman is shrouded in mystery. It can be seen in its glass case and it is not, of course, made of emeralds. The statue is about 70 cm high, and may be made of jade or jasper—no one knows which. No photography is allowed within the temple, so going is the only way you'll ever see it.

This compound, more than any other, will encapsulate for you the magnificence and exoticism of all that is essentially Thai.

The complex is open every day from 8.30 to 11.30am and from 1 to 3.30pm. It is closed on official holidays and entry is 50 baht on weekdays, but free at weekends, when some of the rooms are closed to the public. On Buddhist holy days, it is open and free for Buddhist ceremonies.

After gasping at all that munificence, scamper across the Pramane Ground to the **National Museum.** This is huge, and packed with examples of the incredible range of beautiful sacred and profane artefacts of Southeast Asia. You can see here a panorama of all the dynasties and ruling kingdoms of Siam, Thailand and the whole range of the Mon-Khmer civilisation which has influenced the country. The museum, which has buildings quite as splendid as the exhibits contained inside them, has more than a thousand pieces, from neolithic times to the present.

It is open every day, except Monday and Friday, from 9am to noon, and from 2pm to 4pm, admission five baht, free on Sundays. There are guided tours every morning, starting at 9.30am from the ticket desk. The English-language tours are:
  Thai Art and Culture—Tuesdays;
  Buddhism—Wednesdays;
  Pre-Thai and Thai Art—Thursdays.

Wat Po, or the **Temple of the Reclining Buddha,** is found just south of the Grand Palace. It is the biggest, oldest and perhaps richest temple in Bangkok, and it is important that you allow plenty of time for this one. It is so packed with objects, buildings, statues, big rooms and small rooms, treasures and sacred images that it really is all rather overwhelming. So take it easy and get to know its wonderful treasures. The temple compound is divided—one section for the monks' living quarters, the other for everything else. It was built by King Rama I nearly 200 years ago and is guarded by 16 huge gates.

This was regarded as the first centre of public education, and some of the objects here are not so much religious as educational. It is still sometimes referred to as 'Thailand's first university'. Most people come here to see the gigantic reclining Buddha, which is the biggest in Thailand. It is a stunning 46 metres in length, 15 metres high, entirely covered with gold leaf and with beautifully inlaid mother-of-pearl feet. There are a number of interesting murals in the same chamber, considered by experts to be among the best such paintings in Bangkok, which give an intriguing glance into the daily life of a former age.

In this compound can also be found the headquarters of the traditional medicine practitioners of Bangkok, and many people come here to consult them.

The building in which the reclining Buddha is found is open daily from 8am to 5pm, admission 10 baht.

You can buy temple rubbings here—many of those for sale elsewhere in Bangkok come from here anyway.

Wat Traimit, or **Temple of the Golden Buddha,** is on the Traimit Road near Bangkok's railway station and reasonably central. This temple has a solid gold Buddha, three metres high and weighing five and a half tons. This gleaming golden image was probably constructed in the Sukhothai period and was discovered entirely by accident. The statue was found hidden inside a covering of stucco, revealed only when the statue was dropped while being moved, splitting the stucco and unveiling the real gold image beneath, which had probably been concealed to keep it safe from marauders.

Wat Arun, or **Temple of the Dawn,** is the one which appears on all the tourist brochures and posters. The central pagoda, 79 metres high, dominates the pictures and looks so good against a sunrise or sunset. The

Open-bill storks at Wat Phailom, Pathum Thani

sunset is reckoned the best, even though the temple is named after Aruna, the Hindu God of the Dawn. This was the royal temple of King Taksin, who also kept the Emerald Buddha here before it was moved across the river by the first of the Bangkok kings. It is best looked at from afar, as its silhouette and shape is so graceful. Close to, the many stages of restoration over the ages show too much and not too well. You can climb the tower by some steep steps, if you feel energetic. Open daily, admission five baht.

Wat Mahathat, or the **Temple of the Great Relic,** is very old, and meditation classes are available here. This temple was built during the reign of King Rama I and houses the Mahachulalongkorn Buddhist University, one of the two highest seats of Buddhist learning in Thailand. Information on Buddhism and classes in English can usually be arranged. On holy days there is a thriving open-air market there and many traditional medicine stalls. The temple is open daily from 9am to 5pm, free.

The temple can be found on Na Phrathat Road between Silpakorn University and Thammasat University.

Wat Phailom is a sanctuary for the open-bill stork, and from December to June thousands of them come to nest here. It is located on the banks of the Chao Phraya River in Pathum Thani province.

Wat Benchamabophit, or the **Marble Temple,** is on Si Ayutthaya Road between Chitrlada Palace and the National Assembly building. Head for this temple in the early morning when Buddhist monks are chanting in the chapel. It is also the time when the Carrera marble is at its best. The building was built in the modern style and designed by Prince Krom Pra Naris, a half-brother of the then king and a gifted architect.

The temple is impressive inside as well as out. It is decorated with shining crossbeams of lacquer and gold, and there are numerous beautiful Buddha images dominating the courtyard. It is open daily until 5pm, free.

Wat Rajanadda, just across Mahachai Road from Wat Saket, behind the Chalerm Thai Theatre, is best known for its charm and amulet market, permanently parked there on stalls. The Thais are great users of amulets, and are willing to pay very high prices for powerful ones. You will find not only images of the Buddha here—also Hindu deities, and some very primitive metal amulets. It is interesting to poke around in, though the temple itself is not very notable.

Other Places of Interest

Jim Thompson's House: It was largely due to the work of Jim Thompson, an American businessman with a great love of Thailand, that the Thai silk industry is in the happy state it is today. Thompson arrived in Thailand at the end of the Second World War and set up what has now turned into a multi-million dollar earner. He had a beautiful Thai-style house built, which is open to the public, who can be conducted around in group tours to see what antiques and artefacts Thompson surrounded himself with. The house is lovely and well worth visiting. It is just a pity that the tours are regimented so that it is difficult to actually linger to enjoy the serenity of the place.

Thompson mysteriously disappeared during a trip to the Cameron Highlands, in the Malaysian jungle, and has never been seen again. There have been all kinds of guesses as to his fate—a heart attack, kidnapped by guerillas, that he was actually a CIA agent with enemies, that he suffered a gall bladder attack and wandered off into the forest—but he is now presumed dead, whatever happened.

Admission to the house is from Monday to Friday, 9am to 4pm, 50 baht.

The house is at the end of Soi Kasemsan 2, across from the National Stadium on Rama I Road.

Snake Farm or Pasteur Institute: If snakes are your thing, you'll love this trip. Take a bus up to the corner of Henri Dunant Road and Rama IV Road, west of Chulalongkorn Hospital. This is actually part of the Thai Red Cross—you can get your cholera and typhoid shots here, pick up rabies treatment and watch the venom being extracted from various poisonous snakes to make antitoxin for treatment of snake bites. Many people die in Thailand every year from snake bites.

Open every day from 8.30am to 4pm, venom extracted at 11am for an

A floating market

audience. Admission 10 baht, plus fee for the camera.

Floating Markets: The Wai Sai Floating Market in Bangkok is a total rip-off. All you see are other tourists, and all that happens is that your guide marches you in and out of shops where he gets a commission and where the assistants get nasty if you don't want to buy. Many people complain about these, so avoid them.

If you really want to see water life, there are plenty of other ways to do it. The best way is to pick up a copy of Veran's thoroughly useful little volume *50 Trips Through Siam's Canals* and follow his very explicit directions for taking delightful and adventurous journeys safely up and down the waterways just around Bangkok. It costs 150 baht, but you will save that on your first morning by avoiding the dreadful tour-guided trips.

A slightly less commercial 'Floating Market' trip—but not much less—is the one up to **Damnoen Saduak** in Ratchaburi. The problem with taking tourists en masse to markets is that the essential character of the market changes as Thais begin to sell stuff to tourists. Not really recommended.

The **Weekend Market** was moved from its old traditional place near the centre of Bangkok while the bicentennial celebrations were being held, but it looks as if it will now never move back into town. It can now be found at Chatuchak Park in front of the Northern Bus Terminal at Phahonyothin Road. It is big and fun, one of Asia's best open-air markets. Worth

Thai boxing

wandering around for the interest alone—pets, clothes ethnic and modern, food, brass and copperware, rattanware, electronics and tapes.

Open Saturday and Sunday from 7am to 6pm.

Thieves Market: Two of these: one at Lang Krasuang on At Sadang Road and the other at Woeng Nakhon Kasem near Chinatown. The first is really for secondhand and unredeemed pawnshop goods, the second for antiques and objets d'art. The rule in both is *bargain hard!*

At the **National Theatre** on Na Phra Lan Road next to the National Museum you can see classical Thai dance dramas from time to time—for schedule, telephone 2215861—and a special display is held on the last Friday of each month at 5pm to demonstrate classical dancing and music.

You can also see classical Thai dancing at the shrine at the corner of the **Erawan Hotel** most days and evenings. The shrine is much frequented by those who have made vows. They give offerings to the images there and pay for a dance to be done to honour the granting of their wishes. It is very pleasant and informal and the air is spicy with incense and full of music. It is free, of course, and visitors are welcome to wander into the shrine area. Just show respect.

There are other dance performances at various hotels and restaurants, usually a selection of classical and folk dances, plus good Thai food. This kind of evening, though, is often somewhat unsatisfactory—good dance and good food together are rather difficult to concentrate upon. A range of restaurants offer this, from the almost top-of-the-market Royal Thai Orchid next to the Oriental to the somewhat cheaper Baan Thai on Soi 32 along Sukhumvit Road.

Thai Boxing: This martial art is done for sport, display and self-defence and involves the use of hands *and* feet, plus elbows, knees, shoulders and any other part of the body which makes a good weapon. It is a rough sport surrounded with a great deal of noise and excitement. If that is what you crave, make for Ratchadamnoen Stadium on Ratchadamnoen Avenue, almost next door to the TAT office, every Monday, Wednesday and Thursday at 6pm and on Sundays at 5pm.

On Tuesday, Friday and Saturday, head for Lumpini Stadium, Rama IV Road, starting at 6pm. One extra bit of excitement comes from the fact that traditional music is played during the bouts. There is usually a lot of gambling on the results too.

The **Siam Society** in Ban Kamthieng, at 131 Soi Asoke (Soi 21) Sukhumvit, could well be worth a visit if you have any interest in the history and culture of Thailand. This is an old house that has been transported all the way down from Chiang Mai as a superb example of Thai country-style building. The house also has a large garden full of Thai flora and fauna and bristling with agricultural and marine tools of the trade. There is also a good library, and you can buy excellent monographs on aspects of Thai culture.

Open daily, except Sunday and Monday, from 9am to noon and from 1pm to 5pm, admission 25 baht.

Nightlife

Sex is what Bangkok is famous for all over the world, and there is plenty of that for sale around the city of fallen angels. No one will stop you going to massage parlours, brothels, clubs and cheap hotels with a person of whichever sex you choose.

However, you might care to give an occasional thought to the fact that very many of the girls working in massage parlours have been sold into bonded labour by their parents and are unable to get out. They are slave prostitutes because their families were too poor to feed them, and they are too poor for any man to marry them. If enjoying yourself at the price of other people's misery is what turns you on, go ahead. Patpong Road is the centre of most of this.

Films are announced daily in the English-language newspapers, but be aware that films from the West are heavily cut and Thai films are pretty mindless on the whole. There are several video cafes where you can eat and watch the latest movies from—usually—America. The food is not expensive and the films are free. Again, check the newspaper, as they tend to come and go.

Where to Eat in Bangkok

There are hundreds of good places to eat, and even the smallest Thai restaurant is likely to have good food. Standards of hygiene are high and you need not worry about the food being clean. It's best to avoid the water in ordinary restaurants, however, since it will almost certainly not be boiled.

All the big hotels have good restaurants, both Thai and other cuisines, but their Thai food is usually doctored down for tourists. No, or few, spices. Some of the places we enjoyed eating in include:

THAI

Chit Pochana, Soi 20 Sukhumvit Road, where the Thais love to eat good Thai food. It has an open-air garden and great food.

Sala Rim Naam, Oriental Hotel, a pricey Thai dance plus traditional Thai banquet evening, very elegant.

Whole Earth Cafe—Thai and vegetarian food, plus good videos, in a very peaceful and agreeable setting at 93/3 Soi Langsuan, Ploenchit Road.

Find the little sidestreets near the Peninsula Hotel and walk up them until you come to a tiny market of food stalls where you can get the most marvellous northern Thai food, cheap and good.

INDIAN

Himali Chacha, 1229/11 New Road, good, modestly-priced and very tasty north Indian food.

EUROPEAN

Nick's Number One, 1 Sathorn Tai Road, used to be terrific, the food is still good but hardly anyone seems to go there now. Still, worth trying your luck.

Metropolitain at 135/6 Gaysorn, with Vietnamese and French food, good stuff, not wildly expensive either.

PIZZA

Pan Pan, Sukhumvit Road, run by a very bossy lady who'll push you into your seat, but the food is good and the sweets and coffee excellent, so if you can take the rather cool service it can be worth it.

Around Bangkok

The Ancient City

About 33 kilometres from Bangkok, the Ancient City is a tourist attraction, sort of old Thailand in miniature. It has reproductions of the most famous buildings and temples from Thai history, set on a ground plan which follows the shape of Thailand itself.

It depends upon your own feelings about such places whether you will

บ๊อตต้อม "อัพ"

BOTTOM'UP

like this one. It has been well done, though, and has many scale models painstakingly put together, including the ten-acre spread of the Prasart Khao Phra Viharn, a Buddhist shrine just across the border in Kampuchea over which the two countries have repeatedly quarrelled. It took four years to make this—and 40,000 tons of concrete for the artificial mountain on which the replica is perched.

One exhibit worth seeing is the Sanpekla Prasart Throne Hall of Ayutthaya. It was recreated from documentary evidence, since the original was ruined and reduced to rubble centuries ago. There is also an entirely wood-carved life of the Buddha which took ten years to complete.

The bus leaves for the Ancient City from Ratchadamnoen Avenue at 7am for the half-day trip, returning at 1pm. Fare and entrance, 200 baht. If you really have no time to go and see the real thing around Thailand itself, I suppose the Ancient City is a reasonable replacement.

Ayutthaya

Here you find the vanished glory which Bangkok has replaced, only 50 kilometres from Bangkok and set in the fertile plain known as the rice bowl of Thailand. Modern Ayutthaya is nothing to speak of, but the ruins speak eloquently of former splendour, even from the fallen stones. The ancient city was founded in 1350 and remained a capital city until it was captured and laid waste by the marauding Burmese in the 18th century.

During the time of its greatest prosperity it was one of the great cities of Asia, and even Westerners travelling here in search of spice and the other treasures of the East saw Ayutthaya and left us accounts of its richness and splendour.

There is little left now but reminders of that long-ago magnificence, but it is still a haunting city. The city is tucked into a sheltering loop of the Chao Phraya River, with a connecting canal closing the loop. Because of this it is possible to tour the environs of the city in a boat, and in fact you can travel all the way to Ayutthaya by boat from Bangkok. It takes more than two hours, so you need a bit of time for it, but it turns an already interesting trip into a fascinating one, and changes the pace down to something more peaceful.

There are a number of things in Ayutthaya that you really should see:

Wat Phra Si Sanphet, formerly the royal chapel, most represents the extravagant and elegant style that has come to be known as the Ayutthaya school of architecture. It was built in the 14th century and is now most famous for the impressive *chedis* and for something which is no longer there to be seen. In 1500, a standing Buddha 42 feet high was erected and covered with 580 pounds of pure gold. The Burmese set fire to the chapel in order to try to get the gold. The gold melted and the building itself collapsed.

Buddha images dominate the Ayutthaya landscape

The **Royal Palace** consists of five groups of buildings and therefore gives a sense of just how huge this place must have been in its flourishing years. The buildings, again, have largely fallen into ruin but the standing walls, pillars and porticoes remain to intrigue and tease the imagination.

The **Pagoda of Sri Suriyothi** is a memorial to the courageous queen who risked her own life to save that of her husband during a great battle between elephant-borne warriors in 1563.

There are a group of ruins that are notable simply because they give indications of the immensity of scale involved in the making of the city of Ayutthaya—the **Wat Phra Maha That,** the **Wat Rajburana** and the **Wat Thammik Raj.** One building, for some reason, survived unscathed during the Burmese incursions and this is the **Wat Na Phra Mane,** opposite the Royal Palace. It has been restored, so you are not seeing it in quite its original condition.

The **National Museum**—Ayutthaya is generously provided with two of these. The main one is the **Chao Sam Phraya Museum,** near the junction of Rojana Road and Si Sanphet Road, and the other is the **Chan Kasem Palace,** which is itself a marvellous example of what it is there to show. It is a 17th century building of royal origin.

Both museums are rich with examples of the golden age of Ayutthaya, and are open daily except Monday and Tuesday from 9am to 4pm,

admission two baht. There are good guides to Ayutthaya available at these museums for 15 baht. You will find them very helpful in sorting out one ruin from another.

Bang Pa-In is usually included in any Ayutthaya trip as it is only about 20 kilometres downriver from the ancient capital. It does have a handsome palace, but the real point of going there is the very pleasant river ride down from Ayutthaya. It is actually a slightly odd royal building reflecting the Thai monarchy's early taste for things European which surfaced during the 19th century, so its style is an intriguing mixture of Thai and the Thai version of European.

Lopburi is another of Thailand's ancient cities, about 100 kilometres from Bangkok and dating from the 6th century. There is not a lot to see, but the outstanding feature of Lopburi is a huge complex of three Khmer-style pagodas, semi-ruined and dating from the 11th century. There are also other ruined Khmer-style edifices scattered around this otherwise undistinguished town.

Khao Yai National Park

This is within a day's trip from Bangkok. For details see the National Parks chapter, page 126.

Kanchanaburi and the River Kwai

Kanchanaburi province is said to be the most beautiful province of all Thailand, and that is a big claim in a country with so many other contenders. But most visitors agree with the claim. Kanchanaburi is pure countryside — most of it anyway. Unpolluted rivers, high mountains, magical caves, the home of the blue sapphire, flowing waterfalls and serene fields stretching away into the distance.

One part of the province is already famed all over the world as the place where the notorious 'Bridge over the River Kwai' was constructed by the wretched soldiers working on the infamous Death Railway of the Japanese during the Second World War. However, it is also becoming well known archaeologically for the neolithic remains at Ban Khao. Among those who love Thailand, it is known for its lovely landscapes and hills.

It takes about two hours to drive to Kanchanaburi province from Bangkok along the 129 kilometres of the westward highway. The first major attraction which the visitor will come to along this route, however, is that of Thailand's oldest city, Nakhon Pathom.

Nakhon Pathom

This ancient city is said to date from 150 BC, and you will know that you are approaching it when the towering monument of the **Phra Pathom Chedi** looms up into the sky, all 380 golden shining feet of it. This

breathtaking Buddhist monument is the tallest in the world, and marks the holiest shrine in all Thailand. This is the city where Buddhism is said to have started in Thailand. The golden colour comes, not from gold itself, but from the highly-glazed golden brown tiles which came from China.

In the outer courtyard of the Phra Pathom Chedi are four viharns, or halls, containing images of the Buddha, very finely painted and unusually designed.

The first structure on this site, which is now inside the *chedi*, is thought to have been built by Mon people and resembles the 3rd century architecture of King Asoka. It was during the reign of Asoka that the first Buddhist teachers came to spread the teachings of the Buddha in the kingdom of Suvarnabhumi, the capital of which was sited where Nakhon Pathom is found today. Later, when the area came under Khmer control, the stupa was repaired and overbuilt in Brahmin style.

During the 1850s, King Mongkut (Rama IV) visited the then ruined *chedi* as a Buddhist monk on pilgrimage. He was so moved by the realisation that this was where Buddhism began in Thailand that he decided to have it rebuilt. He also thought that there would undoubtedly be Buddhist relics inside the stupa. He did not live to see the restoration completed.

For the monument-minded, there are other sites to visit around Nakhon Pathom:

The *chedi* in **Wat Phra Pathom** is the second largest in the area, with a 20-metre high structure on a hillock.

Wat Phra Meru has a collection of five-metre high stone Buddha images, the most beautiful of which have been installed in the main shrine hall of the Phra Pathom Chedi.

Sanam Chan Palace, about two kilometres west of the Phra Pathom Chedi, was built in the reign of King Rama VI. It is an odd group of buildings, English architecture with a heavy Thai touch. This was once Rama VI's holiday palace.

An annual fair takes place during November in the grounds of the Phra Pathom Chedi. It is both a religious and secular event. People crowd into the temple and its grounds and there are vendors of fruit and foodstuffs, all kinds of fortune-tellers, musicians, monks and pilgrims. It is a very colourful occasion.

Kanchanaburi

The town of **Kanchanaburi** is situated at the point where two tributaries, the Kwai Yai and the Kwai Noi, meet and form the Mae Klong River. The town of Kanchanaburi itself is not very old. It was built by King Rama III in 1833 and really does not hold many attractions for the visitor, other than a pleasant stroll along the river bank.

Most people, of course, visit Kanchanaburi for one reason—to see the notorious railway bridge. Although the Death Railway was already well known, it was the film *Bridge on the River Kwai,* loosely based on true events, which highlighted this wretched period in history and told the story to millions. Many of the visitors come to see the bridge and to visit the war cemeteries nearby. Increasingly, however, others are now coming for the beauties of the area, and for the Erawan National Park and Sai Yok Waterfall.

The Bridge over the River Kwai: The war memorial can be found about four kilometres from the Tourism Authority of Thailand (TAT) office in town, on the banks of the Kwai Yai River just before it joins the Kwai Noi to become the Mae Klong. The bridge was brought from Java by the Japanese army and was put together by prisoners of war to be part of the railway linking Thailand with Burma. It is estimated that more than 16,000 Allied prisoners-of-war died during the construction of the railway, and an even more appalling 49,000 slave labourers from the Japanese-occupied countries. The bridge was destroyed several times in the final year of the war but was rebuilt afterwards. Of the present structure, only the curved spans are from the original.

There are two war cemeteries in the area, the **Kanchanaburi War Cemetery** in the town itself and the smaller **Chong Kai War Cemetery.** There are 6,982 graves of PoWs in the Kanchanaburi cemetery, all of whom died on the Death Railway. They were brought to Thailand, mostly on foot, by the Japanese from Singapore, Indonesia and Malaysia. They included Dutchmen, Americans, British, Australians, New Zealanders and Canadians. The Chong Kai Cemetery is small, peaceful and carefully tended, with many beautiful flowers and shrubs. Here are the graves of 1,750 PoWs.

The best way to reach Chong Kai Cemetery is to go by boat, either from the pier in front of the town gate or from a boat agent at the Kwai Bridge.

Kao-Poon Cave: About one kilometre away from the Chong Kai War Cemetery is this cave which houses many beautiful Buddha images. It is a bit of a climb but well worth it—for the stalagmites and stalactites as well as the images.

Kao Phang Waterfall: The Death Railway ends at Namtok Station, some 77 kilometres from Kanchanaburi, and two kilometres on you will find the Kao Phang Waterfall. The trip takes you through some of the countryside which amply demonstrates exactly why so many regard this as the most beautiful part of Thailand.

You can picnic and swim at the waterfall. It is best to aim to do this during the rainy season from May to August, otherwise the water level is low.

A regular bus runs from Kanchanaburi to the Kao Phang Waterfall.

Kaeng Lawa Cave and Sai Yok Waterfall: This trip will give the visitor

The bridge on the River Kwai

a chance to view some of that beautiful unspoiled countryside from the river. It is a trip well worth taking if you have about five hours to spare and would like a little adventure. The River Kwai is edged by greenery and forest and you may be lucky enough to see some of the wildlife that lives undisturbed here. The Kaeng Lawa Cave is the biggest around this area and boasts some impressive stalactites and stalagmites. From there you can go on upriver to the waterfall.

The best place to hire a boat is from Pak Saeng pier at Tambon Tha Saow. At the time of writing it cost around 1,000 baht per boat, seating twelve people. The trip takes about two-and-a-half hours upstream and one-and-a-half down.

River Kwai Resorts

Because of the popularity of the River Kwai trip for visitors from Bangkok, there has been considerable holiday-style development all around the area. Obviously it is touristic, but most people appreciate the rural peace and the quiet serenity of the river itself, as well as a chance to stay far from civilisation and city life. Not that this is uncivilised—it is a very pleasant place to stay for one or several days. There are various possibilities for the visitor.

River Kwai Farm: Very attractive — bamboo houses and rafts where guests can stay. Surrounded by nature, food fresh from the farm, this is one for those who long for peace and quiet. It is 32 kilometres from Kanchanaburi, so you need your own transport, or arrange something through River Kwai Farm Company, 16/6 Soi Pipat, Silom Road, Bangkok, Tel: 2330940 or 2356433.

Floatel Rafthouse: Near the Sai Yok Waterfall, these are also rafthouses for visitors. Contact either East-West Tour or Floatel Limited in Bangkok, Tel: 2510179, 2515520 and 3923641.

River Kwai Village Hotel: This is a 60-room lodge, designed in Thai style to international standards of comfort. Very pleasant, with air-conditioned restaurant, bar and private waterfall. More de luxe than the others but just as rural.

It is possible to take a variety of arranged tours from most of the accommodations above — trips to country villages, caves, trekking on elephant back and visiting hilltribe or minority villages.

Erawan National Park: The base for this park may well have been laid down in the 17th and 18th centuries when plantations of bamboo were established, but now it consists largely of deciduous forest with patches of evergreens.

The real attraction here, however, is the Erawan Waterfall, a stupendous cascade. The rock above the waterfall is shaped like a three-headed elephant, hence the name Erawan, which is the name of this mythological creature.

There are seven levels to the falls, with deep emerald green pools of cool water in which to swim, as well as picnic places. This park also boasts considerable wildlife, from elephants to exotic birds, plus — for bat lovers — the natural underground cathedral of the Phrathat Cave, with its multicoloured rock formations ... and bats, of course.

The park has nine bungalows, two dormitory-style houses for 40, plus a camping ground. You can reach it by taking a bus from Kanchanaburi to the market place near the park. Hire a minibus to cover the last two kilometres. You can also hire a minibus all the way from Kanchanaburi, which is 65 kilometres south. Warning: literally hundreds of thousands of Thais visit the waterfall annually. Best avoid weekends unless you want to have an awful lot of company.

River Kwai Family Camp: This is situated just seven kilometres outside Kanchanaburi and is a country vacation spot offering not only accommodation but also a wide range of activities — horseback riding, canoeing, fishing, swimming, carriage riding and trips to interesting places like caves, hill-climbing and even raft trips on the river, at a week's notice.

For reservations either write direct to Mrs Lee Rhodes, Box 20, Kanchanaburi 71000, or contact Vasu Travel Service, between Sois 7 and 9, Sukhumvit Road, Bangkok, Tel: 2511859, 2519237-8.

Getting There

Kanchanaburi: Buses, aircon and non, from Southern Bus Station in Charansanitwong Road, Thonburi, every half an hour, taking about 2½ hours. Details: call 4110511/4110112 (non-air) and 4114978-9 (aircon). Trains, three times daily from Thonburi Station, Bangkok Noi. Details: call 4113102.

There are also special tourist trains on Saturday, Sunday and public holidays, from Bangkok Railway Station, Tel: 2237010.

The East Coast

The east coast of Thailand is, like so many other parts of the country, beautiful. It has a superb coastline, mountains, beaches, islands, waterfalls and many natural delights, plus development for tourism. While that may sound bad to purists, there is no getting away from the fact that it makes visiting there easier and better for visitors.

Chonburi is less than 100 kilometres from Bangkok along the excellent Bang Na to Trat highway. It is right on the sea, as well as being a centre of major agricultural production—sugarcane, tapioca, coconuts—and a marine industry.

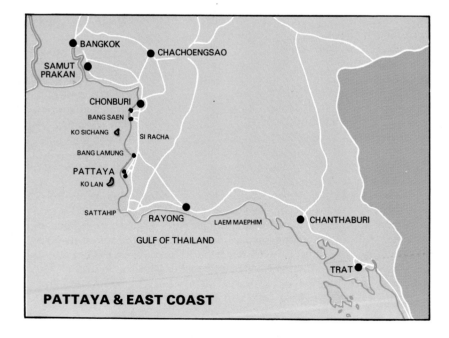

PATTAYA & EAST COAST

Elephants at work in the timber industry

It is a lively town, and there are a number of spots worth visiting around this area, although most tourists will not be much interested in Chonburi itself. Before rushing through it on your way to more romantic or more serene beach towns and villages, stop and look at the **Wat Intharam** near the market in the town centre. It is the most important temple in the province, and the oldest. It looks old too, with some of its features worn away or ruined and a distinctive Ayutthaya air about it. It has some interesting porcelain decorations as well as good frescoes dating from the 18th century.

Ang Sila is a little village about five kilometres south of Chonburi where the Thai royal family used to take their seaside vacations. It is here that the mortars and pestles of every Thai kitchen probably come from, and it is also known for its weaving industry. On the top of a nearby hill is a shrine, the **Chao Mae Sam Muk,** in the shape of a huge ship's hull. Many of the numerous resident population of meditators are Chinese in origin and Chiu Chow is the language mainly in use.

Bang Saen Beach, further down the road, is a favourite of Thai tourists, so if you go there, especially at the weekend, you will have plenty of company. The place is full of vendors and food stalls, tyres to rent for floating on and chairs to rent for browning on. It is good for a one-day seaside trip out of Bangkok, and you can play golf nearby too.

If fish are your thing, take a side trip to the **Marine Zoological Museum,** attached to the Bang Saen campus of Srinakharinwirot University, for the marine aquarium, the zoological museum, natural history museum and an extensive shell collection. Open daily from 9am to 4pm, free.

Look at the **Nong Mon** central market in Bang Saen for good fruit, seafood, sweets and rattanware from the surrounding district.

The **Khao Kheo Open Zoo** can be found about 20 kilometres further along the Bangphra Road. This covers some 1,200 acres and has more than fifty species of wildlife roaming freely within spacious compounds.

For more nature, continue along a left turn beside the Wat Khao Mai Dang and proceed seven kilometres to the **Chan Ta Then Waterfall,** which is an educational centre for studying wildlife and nature in this particularly fresh and scenic area.

Si Racha, 24 kilometres south of Chonburi, is a popular seaside resort, full of sunshine, beach and fresh fruits, with long piers which trickle down into the sea. It is famous throughout Thailand for the hot red sauce which bears its name.

Offshore about 12 kilometres, you can visit the island of **Ko Sichang.** It is quite large, but the only transportation is in the form of bicycles and trishaws, so it has a peace which many visitors will relish. The one big building you will find there is the summer palace King Rama V used to recover from sickness. There are also two temples dating from the same period, one with a chapel and a European-style pagoda. There is also a fine Chinese pavilion. In the **Chakrapong Cave** is a narrow passage through which you can scramble up to get a great view of the surrounding seascape. On the opposite side of the island are the round stones found on **Hin Klom Beach.** They have been made that way by the constant strong winds on that side of the island which have rubbed them up against each other.

The best way to see all these things, if you are too lazy to stroll around, is to hire a trishaw and do the whole lot in about an hour. It is comparatively expensive, however.

The ferry service to the island operates from two of Si Racha's piers, the Ko Loi and Cherm Chompol piers. It starts at 8.30am and stops at 3pm.

A tiny seaside resort can be found further down the highway at **Hat Pa Dang,** or Red Cliff Beach. This is really a Thai place, and it is pleasant and rather less commercial than the other resorts you may come across. There is a swimming pool, some golfing facilities and Thai food and entertainment.

Then, of course, comes Pattaya.

Pattaya

Pattaya is Bangkok's seaside playground. It offers sand, sea and sports of all kinds, including those of the bedroom. It is the kind of place which many people like to describe as spoilt, but that depends upon your viewpoint. In tourism terms it still offers a pleasant seaside holiday, with a wide range of accommodation and restaurants at prices for all but the meanest pockets. The beach is quite good, and the very much better ones are much further away down south. It is true that there are a huge number of bars, clubs and prostitutes—male, female and in between—but somehow it is still a friendly and agreeable place. Some people think it is very raunchy, but the sexual scene seems fairly amiable. At least the prostitutes working around Pattaya are freelancers, and not girls who have been sold as virtual slaves by their parents. And the women in the bars are just as friendly to women as they are to men, in a non-sexual sense, so a couple need not feel any embarrassment in going to such places together.

It does, apart from the bar side of life, make a very good place for a holiday. It has only been developed in the last two decades, before which it was a sleepy little fishing village. Now it is a fully-fledged holiday resort. It has a palm-fringed beach, plenty of people to bring you added comforts in the form of sun umbrellas, sunbathing chairs, massages and cold drinks, a couple of beautiful and fairly undeveloped coral islands with good snorkelling available, and a range of rather more exciting sports like water-skiing, hang-gliding, parasailing, water pedalling and wind-surfing.

Dozens of luxury buses leave Bangkok daily for Pattaya, and the 150-kilometre journey takes from two to four hours, according to road conditions. It is also possible to transfer straight from Bangkok's International Airport at Don Muang to Pattaya, for those who want to avoid even an overnight stay in the city. There are many hotels, offering more than 7,000 luxury class rooms, not to mention many other equally convenient but less luxurious hotels and guest houses for smaller pockets.

The beach is curved and indented and therefore it is always possible to find a reasonably sheltered stretch, especially if you are prepared to walk or ride a bit further on to one of the adjoining beaches reachable at low tide. The main beach is three kilometres long. The next beaches are Palm Beach, Rock Cottages and Moonlight Beach. These are much more sheltered, and you can find bungalows and beach houses for hire there. It is only at weekends that Pattaya is crowded—and when the American fleet is in, of course.

At the time of writing these were the prices operative for the various kinds of water sports activities:

Water skiing—up to 600 baht per hour;
Water scooters—200 baht per hour;
Parasailing—up to 250 baht a sail;
Rent of 14ft Hobie Cat—200 baht per hour;
Rent of 16ft Hobie Cat—250 baht per hour;
Wind surfing—150 baht upwards;
Diving, without equipment—400 baht plus boat rental plus guide;
Diving with equipment—500 baht plus boat rental;
Boat rental—500 baht upwards;
Guide—500 baht.

There are three little islands just off Pattaya which are recommended for those who like peace and quiet—**Ko Lan, Ko Lin** and **Ko Khrok.** Ko Lan is also often called **Coral Island,** and it is the most attractive of the three. You can hire a boat to go there—a small boat with 12-person capacity costs anything up to 1,500 baht. Making life a little easier, though inevitably more commercial, is the fixed tour to Ko Lan, described as the Coral Island Tour by its various operators. This is an excursion trip to the island, and includes a seafood lunch and the use of a glass-bottomed boat to view the coral gardens while you are there. This tour sets off in the morning, usually around 9.30, and returns in the late afternoon. The cost is 280 baht per person.

The tour is the best solution if you are alone, but in a party you can do better by striking a bargain with one of the local boatmen. It takes just under an hour to get there, although you could take a speedboat if time were that much of the essence. There are plenty of little foodshops with deliciously fresh seafood—crabs, prawns, mackerel. You can also stay overnight, either camping or in a hotel or guest house. There is also a golf course, and the best swimming for coral gazing is off the south of the island. Many experienced swimmers and snorkellers advise wearing a T-shirt to protect yourself from the sun's burning rays while you are in the water. The deceptive coolness may conceal the extent to which you are being burned.

Ko Lin, an hour further on, also has good diving, with even some sunken wrecks as attractions, and it is less developed.

Nong Nooch Village

This is a country park, complete with small museum, flower gardens, cactus nursery and orchid garden, boating lake and other distinctly touristic developments. There are cultural displays also, of Thai boxing, Thai dancing, cock-fighting and so on. Some considerable imagination has been shown in the making of the garden, and it is much better than you might expect, but it is pure tourism. It is most popular with Chinese visitors from Hong Kong, Taiwan and Singapore. It is about 20 kilometres out of Pattaya, and you can drive yourself or go on a tour.

Eating Out in Pattaya

There are many good places to eat in Pattaya at many different price levels, but here are some that we especially enjoyed:

Nang Nual on the main street, a fresh seafood restaurant. Beware! Some very persistent young ladies try to sell you fresh fish from little stalls just inside the entrance of the restaurant, but once you get inside to your table the same fish is much cheaper to order off the menu. It just seems to be on of those little rip-off tricks. Refuse to order anything until you have sat

The orchid is Thailand's national flower

down and obtained the menu. The young ladies get very sulky about this, but it doesn't matter because they are not your waitresses anyway. They are, it seems, fishwives. Once you get past these pretty little gorgons, you will have a very pleasant meal.

Dolf Riks' Restaurant, moved from its old traditional place down to south Pattaya, offers excellent European food and good company, and always has done. It is a long-time favourite with those who have frequented Pattaya down the years. Not the cheapest, but worth it. You can also get good Indonesian dishes from Dutchman Mr Riks.

Coral Reef in the main street has good seafood but is only open during the high season. So although its reputation is good, we could not try it.

Pizza Hut, main street. Yes, it does seem awful to have pizzas when there is all that good seafood, but then these are also good pizzas.

Thai food—the best places are the small stalls in the back streets, but be sure that you bargain for the food or you may be overcharged. This is prime tourist territory, so expect the worst if you don't defend yourself.

Rayong

If you think Pattaya is altogether too disreputable or too commercial or too anything for your taste, relax and head on down the road to quieter and more truly Thai Rayong. This is an undeveloped—well, almost—

seaside town, a grown-up version of a Thai fishing village. You'll know that by the smell which will announce itself to your nose—a fierce, demanding, salty pungency that reminds you that this is where *nam pla* comes from. *Nam pla* is a much loved and very intensely concentrated sauce made from fermented fish, and Rayong is where they ferment it.

Beyond is **Ban Phe,** a busy little port where you can see—and smell—bright orange shrimps drying out in the sun. Offshore is the island of **Ko Kaeo Phitsadan,** to which a famous Thai poet retired in the early 19th century to compose his works. It takes only about 30 minutes to get to the unspoiled peace of the white sandy beaches of the island.

There are few concessions to Western-style tourism along this part of the coast, so if you have a sense of adventure and enjoy the simple life, this is the place for you.

Chanthaburi

Chanthaburi is a gem centre, and consequently has a certain casino air about it. Both sides of the main street—not very main—are lined with gem shops, polishing stones, especially the sapphires which come from this area. Star sapphires are the specialities of the place, and you can buy them here for very reasonable prices compared with elsewhere—provided you know what you are buying. Gem buying is a pursuit fraught with dangers for the uninitiated, so be careful.

If you want to see the actual mining being done, take a trip to **Khao Phloi Waen,** which means the 'Hill of the Sapphire Ring'. Open pit mining is the order of the day, and there are men everywhere ready to strike a bargain with you. Just be sure you don't pay too heavily.

Outside the fruit markets of Chanthaburi, where the famous durian can be obtained, there are two waterfalls worth seeing: **Nam Tok Khao Krathing,** in a small national park cascading over a series of small falls, and **Nam Tok Phriu,** with clear pools for swimming.

The other attraction of Chanthaburi is a wide range of hand-woven crafts, many of them made in small cottage industry enterprises in which individual families take part.

Trat

Trat province, the easternmost province of Thailand, is exceptionally beautiful, full of lush green landscapes, offshore islands with large, still lagoons and unstripped seabeds rich with coral and tropical fish. Very few people go there, and it remains a wonderfully kept secret. Go there and find out its hidden delights for yourself.

A Northeastern rice farmer

The Northeast: the Heartland of Thailand

This is both regarded as the real Thailand, where the deepest heart of Thai culture is to be found, and as the supply line for cheap labour for Bangkok. That tells you a lot about the paradoxes of the least developed and mostly purely Thai part of the country. Other Thais refer to this area as E-san, and it is a vast agricultural bowl, subject to both the wicked whims of rising rivers and to the quirks of nature which can keep or destroy the fertility and richness of the land. Industry has yet to make its mark up here, and many of the poor farmers and farm labourers go to Bangkok to find work between harvests, or even instead of harvesting if the year has been hard enough. Most of the dark-skinned young women in headscarves and young men in denim doing lowly labour in Bangkok—on building sites, in the waterways and around the markets—come from the poor Northeast. Half of the girls in the massage parlours of Thailand come from here, many of them sold into bonded labour—virtually becoming slave prostitutes—by parents too poor and desperate to support them.

Few tourists venture here, and therefore facilities are few in number. It is not pretty Thailand, with willing service eager to spoil the visitor, and yet if you really want to know something about the country and its real problems and aims today, this is where you go. There are actually some interesting tourist attractions too.

There have been heartening developments. The Friendship Highway, built by Thai-American money, now serves as a link that enables the farmers of the Northeast to send their produce to Bangkok. Dams have been built, electricity is arriving in the villages and life is slowly—for some, too slowly—improving.

Nakhon Ratchasima (Korat)

This is the capital of the Northeast, a commercial, communications and military centre. It grew rapidly during the 1960s, when it was a centre for American forces operating in the Vietnam war. Although the city is passably equipped with the pleasantnesses of modern life, its main attractions lie outside the urban area.

At **Pak Thong Chai,** some 27 kilometres to the south, is the centre of the silk thread industry which supplies the silk weaving factories of Bangkok.

Phimai, some 44 kilometres distant, is one of the most spectacular of the numerous great temples of the Northeast. Most of them are thought to be at least a thousand years old and are of two types—three to five-storeyed bases built by Brahmins and low-based structures built by Buddhists.

Very little is known about the towering temple of Phimai. One expert dates it from the 12th century, just before Angkor Wat, while another sets it in the reign of King Surijavoram (AD 1002-1049). It was thought to be built by Mahayana Buddhists, and no one knows how it fell into ruins— whether by natural disaster or at the hands of man.

Phu Kradung National Park in the province of Loei was one of the first and most beautiful of all the national parks of Thailand. It covers about 348 square kilometres and is a single sheer-sided mountain covered with evergreen forest. Its name means Bell Mountain, and one tale claims that it has this name because a mysterious bell-like note comes from the mountain on each Buddhist holy day. Another more prosaic explanation is that the name merely refers to its shape, which is a mountain rising into a vast elevated plateau, teeming with wildlife.

Among the wildlife are wild pigs, wild dogs, giant squirrels, gibbons, Asiatic black bears, deer and many kinds of birds. There is a trail leading up the mountain, at times very steep indeed. Walk up in time for sunrise for an unforgettable experience, but be sure to take plenty of warm clothes whatever time of year you go. It is about 4.5 kilometres from base to summit and you should allow four hours, because the path is tough. There are spectacular views as you approach the summit. Between October and January the place is booked up with Thai students, and remember not to go in the wet season, as you may slide all the way back down again.

There is very limited accommodation, and you absolutely must book in advance. The information available at the park is only in Thai, and English is not spoken by anyone there, so for this one you really must get the National Parks Guide issued by Shell.

There are not nearly as many *wats* in the Northeast as elsewhere — perhaps due to lack of money to build them — but one worth a visit is the **Wat Tamkhong Paen,** about 90 kilometres from Loei on the Udon Thani road. The temple is built among huge rock formations and is very peaceful, while the monks' meditation huts are actually perched on, in and around the rocks.

Chiang Khan is a small frontier town edging the Mekong River, the water border between Thailand and Laos. You can hire a boat here for a four-kilometre ride downstream to the Kuang Kud Ku rapids, a heart-stopping experience.

The town itself is largely Chinese, and its quiet side streets are lined with the old-style wooden houses which used to grace the countryside and town before the onslaught of concrete. It is a pleasant place to stop and relax in.

If you don't want to pay the price of a boat ride to the rapids, then take a *samlor* and bargain hard about the fare before you agree to get in.

Udon Thani is a sad sample of what concrete and too many foreign servicemen can do to what was perhaps once a fairly agreeable town. It is full of bicycle trishaws and you will be pestered all the time by them. It really has nothing much to recommend it.

Ban Chiang has become famous as the place in Southeast Asia where the oldest known human artefacts are to be found. Long before this discovery was ratified by academics, villagers had long been used to turning up shards of pottery, beads and bones, but it was only in the 1960s that these were confirmed as being between 7,000 and 8,000 years old. This may yet prove to be where civilisation began. Do not buy things from the villagers, as you will not be allowed to take them out of the country and you could also risk prosecution. Ban Chiang is a little beyond Udon Thani.

Nong Khai, once a charming little riverside town, lost half its charm when it was no longer possible to cross the Mekong on the little ferry boat and head for **Vientiane** in Laos. However, if you have a lucky day and catch the Laotian Embassy in Bangkok in an agreeable mood, you may well get a visa to go as far as Vientiane, but no further. If you can do that, you will find that Vientiane still has some of the character that made it famous in more raucous times than now. And it still has quiet tree-lined roads, a huge and bustling morning market and monks about the streets. It also has some of the trappings of Asian communism — loudspeakers on lamp-posts and a certain amount of regimentation.

Surin has become something of a tourist trap since the TAT started organising a so-called **Elephant Roundup** there every November. The people of Surin were famed for their ability to handle elephants, and the

three-day roundup has become a cross between a carnival and a rodeo. If you like to see elephants playing football, this is your chance. The actual roundup is not an actual roundup at all. All the elephants involved in it are already tamed and being trained, so it is more of a staged display for the shutterbugs. Many people love it, so who am I to argue with them? If you want to go, book well ahead, as it is impossible to get into Surin around that time without booking. You can travel there from Bangkok while the event is on.

Chiang Mai and The North

Chiang Mai, Thailand's second largest city, is known as the Flower of the North, and it deserves the title. Not only does it boast—so say the Thais—the prettiest girls in Thailand, but it has many other beauties too. It has superb handicrafts both in and around the city, with plenty of interesting ways to visit them. Using Chiang Mai as your base, you can go deep into the countryside, up into the hills where orchid-laden trees clothe the rocky slopes across which you must travel to visit the hilltribes people in their villages. You can visit national parks where the lush green landscape has become a sanctuary for wildlife in the area. You can go

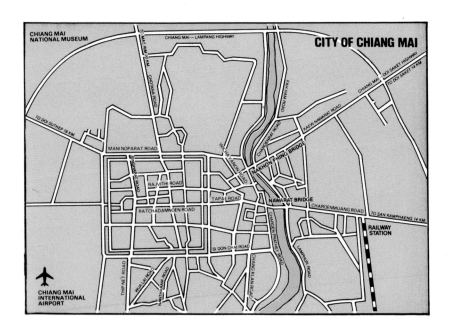

trekking for one day or for three weeks. You can take a river raft and float past stunning waterfalls and soaring rock walls. There is more to do in and around Chiang Mai than the average visitor ever finds time for.

The city itself is not what you might expect. It is rather more of a country town in which the traffic has taken over—roaring motorbikes, heavily panting *samlors*, labouring trucks—and seems at first glance to have gobbled up all the quiet charm which you can easily see used to belong to Chiang Mai. However, once you have spent a little time wandering around you will begin to find that it does indeed still have considerable interest, even though its charms have perhaps been indelibly stained by modernisation and over-development in which real aesthetic or architectural values have played no part.

It is the only city in the North capable of supporting tourism of any real standards, and it does make a natural centre from which to go out to other places. It is also easy to get to from Bangkok, and you have many ways to travel to Chiang Mai. You can get there from Hong Kong, the only international connection with Chiang Mai—a direct flight, three times weekly. From Bangkok there are at least five flights daily, some direct and some via other destinations.

For those who enjoy train travel, there are excellent rail connections with Bangkok. Several trains leave every day, but most travellers prefer the overnight express which leaves Bangkok at 6pm and arrives early next morning in Chiang Mai. Good value on the train is the second class sleeper, which is reasonably priced and comfortable, with bunk bed, linen and washing and toilet facilities. You can also buy meals which are passable and very cheap.

Cheaper still are the buses. Dozens leave Bangkok every day for Chiang Mai. The level of the fare varies with the level of the quality. Cheapest and worst are the government non-airconditioned buses, in which you will be lucky if you are not sitting next to a broken window. Next best come the government airconditioned and best of all and most expensive—but still cheaper than the trains—are the private luxury tour buses with airconditioning, clean toilets, maybe even a video show and meal stops. Before your journey, check whether the bus makes meal stops. Not all do, and you will have to take your food on with you or get very hungry along the way.

Warning: It is only fair to point out that some buses have been stopped and robbed, which is why Thais may encourage you to take trains. However, statistically you stand a very good chance of not being robbed. As a helpful note, government non-airconditioned buses are virtually never robbed, while private luxury buses are—draw your own conclusions about the reasons for that. Should the worst happen, do not attempt to resist. Losing money is an unfortunate incident, but losing your life is an irreversible disaster.

Chiang Mai is some 700 kilometres from Bangkok, and it has had a very different history. It is virtually as old as the Thai race itself, dating back to 1298. In the 13th century, the Thais fled from southern China and a Thai kingdom was set up around Chiang Rai by King Mengrai. After forming additional liaisons with other local rulers, King Mengrai founded a new capital at Chiang Mai in 1298. He built a city with walls and a moat, and it flourished for a hundred years or so. After that wars between the different tribes meant that Chiang Mai was surrounded by enemies, and gradually that first flourish of power faded.

Fighting and trouble dogged Chiang Mai until the 18th century, when it came under the aegis of the kingdom of Siam and peace was re-established. The present moat dates from that time but moat, walls and gates have all been subject to considerable and necessary reconstruction. However, some of the temples to be found in the city today do indeed date from the time of its glory and are well worth a visit.

There are, for the numerically minded, said to be some 300 temples in and around Chiang Mai, but only a few are so outstanding that they should not be missed. A wonderful time of day to visit temples is at sunrise or, if you cannot manage that, at sunset. Take a trishaw and tour the four or five major temples.

Wat Chiang Man: Historically the most important temple in the city, this was built at the command of King Mengrai, who was said to have lived in it until the city of Chiang Mai was completed. It dates from 1296, although it has been restored and modified since then. There is a relic monument—a *chedi*—at the back of the temple, a northern Thai stupa with elephant supports, and two special images kept within the temple which can only be seen with permission from the abbot. One is a bas-relief known as the **Phra Sila** which is said to have been offered to King Mengrai by monks from Sri Lanka. It is thought to be of 8th century Indian origin. The other is the Crystal Buddha—**Phra Sak Tang Tamani**—said to be a 5th century figure. The people of Chiang Mai revere it for its rain-making abilities and its power to keep evil spirits away.

Wat Chet Yot: Just northwest of the old walled city, near the Chiang Mai Museum, this temple was built in 1455 by King Tilokorat, whose ashes were buried there. It celebrated the 2,000th year of the Buddhist Era, and the chief attraction there is the seven-spired *chedi*. The whole temple is a replica of the Buddhist monument at Bodh Gaya in India, the place where the Buddha became enlightened. Twenty years after it was built, this temple was the seat of the 8th Buddhist Council which revised the teachings of the Buddha. Much of it has been conserved and reconstructed by the Thai government.

Wat Suan Dok: The Flower Garden Monastery, which was the site of a royal pleasure garden in the 14th century. It was later donated to the Buddhists by another king and became a famous shrine. There are relics

stored inside the stupa, but poor restoration has spoiled the look of the temple. A Buddha statue dating from 1504 can be seen there—so, too, unfortunately can a huge cement worship hall.

Wat Phra Singh Luang: This is the most famous temple in Chiang Mai, and it was founded in 1345. The main shopping street in Chiang Mai, Ratchadamnoen, stops just where the temple is to be found. The name of the temple comes from that of the most famous image in northern Thailand, the Phra Singha Buddha, which is housed in a charming old chapel to the left and slightly behind the main buildings. There are also some northern Thai narrative murals in the chapel showing episodes from Buddhist writings. They portray 16th century Thai clothing and customs. To the right of this chapel is a carved wood facade which is a splendid example of craftsmanship, and the decorated porch is another example of fine Thai architecture. The image is well worth seeing, and is a favourite focus for Buddhist worshippers in Chiang Mai.

Wat Chedi Luang: This huge ruined stupa, the main entrance of which is on the Phra Pok Kao Road, is the biggest relic or *chedi* in northern Thailand. This impressive example of Chiang Mai's golden age was built in 1391 by King Saen Muang Mai and extended by King Tiloka, but—sadly— was badly hit during an earthquake in 1545. What remains still gives a good impression of what it once must have been like, and the assembly hall is thought to be one of the most beautiful examples of Chiang Mai monastic architecture. The city's foundation stone and guardian stands beneath an old Bo tree just inside the monastery.

There are many other temples, and if you enjoy temple spotting, include **Wat Duang Di**—a small temple behind the law courts with two beautifully carved wooden pediments but badly damaged walls; **Wat Ku Tao**—out of the city by White Elephant Gate, then right at 100 metres, pass a ruined *chedi* then on to a narrow path which leads to this Burmese-style temple; **Wat Pa Pao** and **Wat Chang Yuen,** both on Mani Noparat Road, the first a rather romantic Burmese-style temple with some interesting architecture, primitive paintings and an air of serenity, and the second a Chinese-style temple with colourful but damaged decorations.

Handicrafts

Chiang Mai is famous, and rightly so, for its handicrafts. Perhaps because of its very different history or for some other less obvious reason, there seems to be a greater range of handicrafts produced in and around Chiang Mai than anywhere else in Thailand. Some of these are indigenous to the province while others were imported by immigrants to the area, and you will then find the craft confined to one place or village and the skill passed down through one family or one closely-knit group.

Among the handicrafts found around Chiang Mai are wood-carving, silverwork, lacquerwork, umbrella-making, weaving, pottery and a small amount of lace-making and basket-weaving.

Wood-carving: The wood most valued by the carvers is teak, and the art of carving it is by no means a new one. Fine examples of religious and secular carving can be seen on many old buildings. Some say that the art was brought to Chiang Mai by the Burmese in the 17th century, but it has now become a commercial craft and wood-carvers can be found all over Chiang Mai, with particular concentrations in Tapae Road and Singharat Road. Products include carved animals and domestic ware, from salad servers to cabinets and tables. Much is exported.

Silverwork: Wua Lai Road is the silversmiths' street, starting near the Chiang Mai Gate and running straight through the silversmiths' district of Ban Wua Lai. Although the official claim is that only pure silver is used, that seems to be a most dubious assertion. However, it is true that the silverware is finely crafted and well designed. From embossed bowls and boxes to intricately worked filigree jewellery, there are many attractions in the silver quarter of Chiang Mai, and with some judicious bargaining and plenty of comparative shopping, most visitors will be pleased with their purchases.

Lacquerware: This is an indigenous craft of northern Thailand, the lac beetle having long been raised on local trees. This ware is called *khoen*, but the actual lacquer these days is often imported black commercial lac from Burma. It is cheaper, but still looks good and its deep black finish comes from lac mixed with pot black. The objects to be lacquered, made of bamboo or teakwood, are first coated with lacquer and then painted with either water-colours or gold. The main lacquerware village can be found behind the Wua Lai Road near the Wat Nantharam south of Chiang Mai. Among the products available are bowls, cups, plates, boxes and trays. The village has really become rather more industrialised and is no longer very picturesque, except that the visitor can at least watch the process of making and decorating the lacquerware.

Umbrellas: The umbrella village of Bo Sang is perhaps Chiang Mai's most famous local craft village. Six kilometres east of town on a flat road — ideal for a lazy bike ride — on the way to San Kamphaeng, there are factories galore here turning out the decorated paper umbrellas originally made by the Chinese. The umbrellas are made of durable waxy paper, cotton or even silk, then hand-painted in many designs of flowers or butterflies. While the umbrellas are pretty enough, the village itself is often something of a disappointment to those expecting picturesque little cottage industrial scenes. It is really more of an umbrella factory, but still worth a visit.

Weaving: Both silk and cotton thread are made in the North and woven into material from which sarongs and other goods are made. The main weaving area is around San Kamphaeng, where there are numerous cottage

industry ventures. Commercial, traditional and machine-operated looms are all employed to make lengths of raw silk and other cloth. Look for these products in the markets of Chiang Mai, and remember to bargain hard for them.

Thai celadon: Thai celadon is a jade-coloured glazed ceramic, based upon that made much earlier during the Sukhothai period of Thai history. This used to be a household craft carried out by immigrant Shan tribe families, but it has become industrialised now and there are several factories in Chiang Mai, of which the most famous two are Kiln of Thai Celadon, six kilometres out of town on the Mae Rim road, and Chiang Mai Sangkalok, five kilometres along the Chom Thong road. Visitors can buy large vases, bowls and pots of all sizes and tea and coffee sets. Beware of alleged antique celadonware, as many excellent fakes are still being manufactured.

Tribal clothing: Brightly-coloured ethnic garments can be found in any of two dozen shops up and down the main roads of Chiang Mai. Although intended for tourists, they are usually made by the actual hilltribes and are more or less based upon tribal costumes. Buy up North, as they will cost you a fortune in Bangkok. Look around, check the quality of the embroidery carefully and then bargain.

Lace: By the old city moat you can find the Sarapee Handmade Lace shop where Dutch-style lacework is produced.

Basket and rattanware: All over northern Thailand the best bargains can be found in the markets where ordinary people buy it. It is handsome stuff, and worth getting. Modest prices.

Markets

There are a number of markets around Chiang Mai, but the one most worth a visit is the **Night Market.** You can find it on the Chang Klan Road, near the junction with Suriwong Road. It starts around 7pm and goes on till around 11pm and you can shop for tribal clothing, handicrafts, lengths of cloth, antiques real or fake and many cheap and eye-catching souvenirs. There is also a range of excellent food stalls, with Thai, Chinese and fresh seafood, but you must establish the cost of each dish before you order, or you could be overcharged. Hygiene is good and you need fear no ill effects.

Beware the **Viang Ping Bazaar,** which is deceptively near where you expect to find the real Night Market. It really is a tourist trap, with the high prices that result from that kind of development.

Books

Two good bookshops grace Chiang Mai. One is the small but well-stocked **Chiang Mai Book Centre** just outside Tha Phae Gate almost

opposite Daret's Restaurant. The other is the larger **Suriwong Book Centre** on Si Don Chai Road, open seven days a week with books, magazines and stationery.

Museums

Chiang Mai National Museum is worth a visit for the Buddha images, among other things. The museum can be found along the Superhighway between the Chotana intersection and the Huai Kaeo Road. It is closed on Monday and Tuesday, open from 9am to noon, 1pm to 4.30pm other days.

Tribal Museum, Tribal Research Centre, Chiang Mai University campus, has some fine examples of tribal silverware, plus traditional lifestyles. This is part of the Tribal Research Centre, where you can get a certain amount of information, but do not expect help with planning your trek. You are unlikely to get it. There is a library attached, but the female staff are unhelpful and apparently uninformed about their stock.

Eating Around Chiang Mai

Eating is a pleasantly rewarding experience in Chiang Mai. There are many and varied restaurants, cafes and food stalls, at any price which suits your pocket. You will soon track down your own favourite eatery, but here are some well-established places on the food trail:

President Hotel, on Wichayanon Road, offers Thai food in airconditioned surroundings at fairly reasonable prices. This is frequented by local Thais, as well as by visitors nervous of less respectable-looking places.

Daret's, near Tha Phae Gate, is probably the restaurant most loved by travellers, and everyone eats in it from hippies—yes, you didn't know there still were any, did you?—to blue-rinsed ladies. Sometimes the service shows this, with a contempt rarely found in Thailand. Still, they do have excellent Chinese and reasonable Western and Thai-style food and legendary fruit smoothies. Lush creamy fruit shakes and ice. Breakfast is good value here too.

Aroon Rai, almost opposite Daret's, has northern Thai specialities like sticky rice, roast chicken and other very tasty dishes.

Whole Earth, on Si Don Chai, serves excellent Thai and Indian vegetarian food in a peaceful and wholesome atmosphere.

Diamond Hotel, on Charoen Prathet, offers a special for visitors—a Lanna Khan Toke dinner in beautiful old surroundings, excellent traditional Thai food and Thai and tribal dancing. A whole evening's entertainment, from 7pm to 10pm.

Street markets and noodle stalls. Look, pick and eat, sitting at a table on the pavement or in a street market. The way the Thais like to eat. Cheap and good. Don't fear dysentery.

Trips out from Chiang Mai

Of course you do not have to base yourself in Chiang Mai, but for the purposes of covering places worth visiting around the North, all these trips are planned out of Chiang Mai since most people do use it as their focal point.

Trekking around Chiang Mai: It would be almost impossible not to think of doing a trek, since every second shop in Chiang Mai seems to be run by a trek tour outfit. The problem is how do you choose the best? Well, first of all, do you really want to do a hilltribe trek or do you want merely to get out into that beautiful Thai countryside, orchid forests and lush rice paddies? It is impossible to get to an unvisited hilltribe village in a trek which takes under four nights—in fact seven nights would be more like it. Every hilltribe village for at least twenty miles around Chiang Mai has been visited, photographed and thoroughly tourist-ridden for at least a score of years. Go there and you will be charged for taking photos—and really, why not? Tribal people are not zoo animals—sold handicrafts the villagers probably bought in Chiang Mai, and even perhaps slightly resented.

The Tribal Research Centre wisely points out that, if you want to get into beautiful countryside and not do a headcount of hilltribes, there are plenty of trips you can organise yourself. With the helpful advice of two of the specialists at the Centre, Mr Somphob Larchrojna and Mr Chira Prangkio, here are some suggestions which you will find equally attractive and which you can do by yourself. These are all safe and scenically magnificent.

Khuntan

This is a one-day trip, starting with a train ride from Chiang Mai to Khuntan, which is between Lampang and Lamphun. Get off at Khuntan after taking the morning train and start off on the four hours of gentle walking which will lead you to the Khuntan Peak. This goes through lush green countryside, and of course gives splendid views of the land below as you steadily ascend. There are three peaks with small guest houses on each should you wish to stay overnight. The best is the guest house known as Yo Sam (Peak Three), a wonderful place from which to watch the sunrise. If you want to return to Chiang Mai the same day, just make sure you catch the early evening train back. Take the ordinary class stopping train.

Doi Inthanon National Park

Doi Inthanon is the national park within easiest reach of Chiang Mai. A 60-kilometre run down the Chom Thong road brings you to the park. Take a look along the roadside at the 16-kilometre mark where basketware

shops line the edge of the road. When you get to Chom Thong, be sure to visit the little monastery there, where you can see some religious relics in a crystal cup.

Doi Inthanon is the highest peak in Thailand, around 8,500 feet, and the park around it is considered to be one of the most beautiful and awe-inspiring in the country. It is full of shadowy forest, hilltribe villagers and a scattering of all kinds of animal and bird life. From the jungle forest to the misty tropical peak, it makes an outstanding trip. You can hire a vehicle to take you up the punishing slopes approaching the peak.

For more details, see **National Parks,** page 126.

Doi Suthep

This is an easy trip to make out of Chiang Mai, and it has the advantage of offering the visitor a chance to see a hilltribe village without having to take an overpriced tour. Obviously, since it is so near Chiang Mai, this is an extremely well-visited village which boasts a number of handicraft shops, but it is still worth going to if you are pushed for time.

Take a bus, minibus or your own transport and head for Chiang Mai University, which is about five kilometres out of town to the west. You will come to a monument of a northern Thai Buddhist monk, Guruba Sri Vijaya or Wichai, which marks the start of the mountain road leading up to the **Wat Phra Doi Suthep.** This is where you can take a minibus to the top, if you do not feel sufficiently energetic to walk all the way. When you hire the minibus, be sure to settle whether it is to be a return trip or not and fix the price accordingly.

The mountain road passes many little pathways leading to beautiful waterfalls—so you can see the advantage of walking. At the top is a Buddhist monastery, with a holy relic enshrined in a 16th century golden stupa. Walk up the 300 steps of the dragon staircase to get there. While you get back your breath and admire the stupa, you will also get a terrific view of the surrounding countryside.

About six kilometres further on you will find the King's summer palace, the **Buping Rajanivesana**, with its landscaped grounds and flower gardens. When the Royal Family are not in residence, the public is allowed to wander around the grounds.

Another three kilometres of rough road brings you to **Ban Doi Pui,** a Meo village. It has been somewhat changed from the typical hilltribe village it may once have been, but you can still see people wearing traditionally colourful dress and rich silver jewellery.

River Trip

Set off from Chiang Mai early in the morning to do this trip. If you are going by bus, take the bus to Chiang Rai, then to Fang. From Fang, which is pretty wild country edging up as it does towards the Golden Triangle territory, take another bus along the rough 24-kilometre road to Thaton. It is a simple journey, even with the bus changes, but wearing, as it bounces over some 170 kilometres of road. At Thaton you can arrange to take a riverboat the five or more hours down the Mae Kok River to Chiang Rai. The last riverboat leaves around noon so that it can be sure of arriving in Chiang Rai before dark. This is due to the recent practice of bandits stopping and robbing the boats. Now every boat has an armed guard on duty throughout the journey.

Apart from the excitement of the boat journey, even without robbers, both Fang and Thaton are in the heart of hilltribe country and you will see many hilltribes people in both towns, especially Yao. Do not worry too much about the possibility of being robbed, but carry as little money and valuables as possible, just in case. This river trip can cost anything up to 2,500 baht if you book it in Chiang Mai and a fraction of that if you take public buses and arrange the boat ride in Thaton. There are usually plenty of spare seats and they go for around 200 baht per person. You do not need a guide to do the trip, as all buses are labelled with their destination in English.

Mae Hong Son

If you really genuinely want to see a great deal of beautiful countryside and do some good trekking, take the advice of the Tribal Research Centre and do the Chiang Mai-Mae Sariang-Mae Hong Son-Mae Taeng-Chiang Mai circuit. You can extend it to include the Thaton-Chiang Rai river trip if you like. You really need seven days for this trip.

Mae Hong Son is 370 kilometres from Chiang Mai, and the bus leaves from Chiang Mai at 7am every day. Obviously you have far more flexibility on a motorcycle or in a car. Mae Hong Son is right up on the Thai-Burmese border, and if you go trekking you will really find yourself in true tropical rain forest so dense that you can scarcely see the sunlight trickling down through the trees. If you want to risk it you can even cross the border, although this is illegal. Most of the hilltribes here are Karen and Shan. Trekking is hard work from here, so be sure you have a very reliable guide and the right equipment, plus extra food. Even if you do not want to trek, Mae Hong Son is well worth a visit anyway. It is a busy market town— by serene old world standards, that is—in the morning and dead by 7pm. High misty mountains loom over the town and it really does feel like the very edge of civilisation.

This trip includes the **Mae Klang Waterfall,** at the entrance of Doi Inthanon National Park, a roaring cataract of brown and foaming water— and highly commercialised.

About 17 kilometres from the delightfully named but featureless town of **Hot,** you find the **Ob Luang Gorge,** libellously described as Thailand's

Karen girl weaving cotton cloth

Grand Canyon. 'Thailand's Little Canyon' would be more appropriate.

Mae Sariang is the last little town on the road before you get to Mae Hong Son, and it has little to distinguish it, except that it signals the start of the most spectacular part of the already breathtaking scenery.

Mae Sae

This is the little border town which joins this part of Thailand officially with Burma, as opposed to all the other somewhat illegal connections. It has a street market in which you can find precious stones—if you know them from glass—some rather fierce Burmese cheroots and other odds and ends brought in by people crossing the border. Unless you are Thai, you will not be allowed to cross into Burma and, as Mae Sae itself is not very attractive and the market not very extensive, there does not seem to be much reason to go there. It is over-romanticised, especially by guides who are trying to sell you a trip there. By bus from Chiang Mai.

Chiang Saen

Now this is more like it. This is the last little town before the officially designated point of the **Golden Triangle,** and it has a really haunting charm of its own. It sprawls along the Mekong River, over on the other side of which are the hills of Laos. It was once an ancient capital, and scholars date its founding back to the 13th century. There are several old stupas edging the town just after you cross the old ramparts, belonging to various monasteries. They are almost in ruins but set serenely under trees, and they have a special atmosphere of their own. There is also a small museum nearby which has some statues and other fine examples of Chiang Saen style.

This is one of the most peaceful towns you are likely to come upon in Thailand, made more so by the river along which the town stretches. It has a couple of hotels, but best of all is the Chiang Saen Guest House, which is very modestly priced and one of the best small guest houses I came across anywhere. The owner of the guest house, Som, can suggest all kinds of trips that you can make.

The Golden Triangle is reachable by the river road. It is about eleven kilometres away, and you can take a minibus, cycle or even walk. You will know when you have arrived at the Golden Triangle by the huge concrete archway which reads 'Welcome to the Golden Triangle'. The misty blue waters where the three countries—Burma, Laos and Thailand—meet is a view which you will find difficult to forget. It has a serenity which the years of drug-smuggling and fighting seem to have left untouched, and it is very hard to imagine that this apparently deserted stretch of the Mekong in a way represents misery for so many people around the world.

Get there by bus from Chiang Mai to Chiang Rai, then from Chiang Rai to Chiang Saen. The route is particularly scenic from Chiang Rai onwards, through forested hills, passing many hilltribes people on the way.

The Hilltribes of Thailand

The hilltribes who are now found scattered in many small settlements in the highlands of western and northern Thailand are tribal minorities who have their origins in China and Tibet. Most of them arrived during the last eighty years or so, following a series of migrations from their original homelands through Asia until they finally reached Thailand.

The hilltribes brought with them a distinctively different lifestyle from that of most Thais, some colourful costumes and a set of beliefs quite separate from those of native Thais.

Poverty is still a characteristic of hilltribe life. The people of the tribes are often less healthy and less educated than others. They keep to their isolated communities away from the mainstream of Thai life, and although this may seem romantic to the visitor who goes to see them in their natural habitat, it is not a situation without problems. Both the style of agriculture pursued by the hilltribes and the nature of their crops can be troublesome. The usual way in which the hilltribes raise their crops is to plant in

different sectors of land each time, which tends to result in deforestation. The fact that a major crop in the past has always been the opium poppy is an aspect of hilltribe agriculture which is no longer acceptable to the Thai government.

As a result of this concern, the government has inaugurated a number of projects in recent years to both help the hilltribes to find other more preferable cash crops and to do something to lift them out of their unfortunate economic position. The biggest of all the projects is the Royal Development Project for the Hilltribes.

The hilltribes fall into two major groups: the Sino-Tibetan group, which includes the Karen tribes, and the Tibeto-Burman group which includes the Lahu, Lisu and the Akha together with the Meo and the Yao. The other major group is of Australasian origin and includes the Lawa (or Lua), H'tin, Khamu and the Mrabri.

The hilltribes commonly found in the low hills and the high valleys are the Karen, the Lawa, the Khamu and the H'tin. They are not the opium growers. Those known for their opium growing are the Meo, the Yao, the Lahu, the Lisu and the Akha. They usually live at 1,000 metres or more because this is the height at which the opium poppy flourishes. All came from southern China.

There are thought to be at least 400,000 hilltribes people, of whom the Karen are the most numerous at around 200,000. The Meo come next, with about 40,000, the Lahu have more than 30,000, the Yao around 25,000 and the H'tin around 20,000. There are just under 20,000 Akha, about 15,000 Lisu, more than 10,000 Lawa and a mere 7,000 Khamu. The most primitive of all—the Mrabri (also called 'the spirits of the yellow leaves' in Thai) are a mere 70 in number.

Most hilltribe villages tend to be organised in largely the same way. They have a headman whose job is to keep an overall eye on the village and its affairs, and apart from the respect given to this man, and possibly to his assistants if he has any, the tribal village is a fairly egalitarian set-up.

Basically, most of the people are animists who believe strongly in the influence of the spirits to be found in the world, many and varied as they are. Each village tends to have at least one man who can perform many spiritual and even medical duties, and this may or may not be the headman.

Having said this as a general introduction, it would probably be useful to start pointing out some of the differences between the various hilltribes and the ways in which they live or the beliefs they hold.

Karen

The Karen (called Yang by the northern Thai people) are the largest group of hilltribes people now settled in Thailand. They came earlier than many of the others, some 200 years ago, after trouble with their Burmese neighbours. They can be found mainly, but not exclusively, living along the Thai-Burmese border.

They are divided into four sub-groups: the Skaw or White Karen, known as such from the fact that unmarried women wear white (in fact, beige to off-white) clothes; the Pwo Karen, or Plong; the Pa-O, or Taungthu (hillmen) and the Bwe or Kayah.

Karen villages are usually found in the lower highlands, around 500 metres above sea level, and their villages tend to be sited in the same place for a long time. Many Karen villages have remained on the same site for more than a hundred years. The people are mainly involved with agriculture, and follow a form of crop rotation, from rice to vegetables. They also raise animals and chickens.

The Karen are also rather different from other hilltribes in that they have a matrilineal kinship line, and their marriages are monogamous and made for life. In religious belief, they were animist and are often now Buddhist, retaining a number of their animistic beliefs as well.

They are commonly found throughout northern Thailand, except in the provinces of Nan and Phrae. They can be found as far south as Tak. They are most numerous, however, on the Chiang Mai to Hot road, on the way to the beautiful Mae Hong Son area near the Burmese border.

Meo

The Meo (often spelt Miao) call themselves the Hmong. They are among the national minorities of China and are commonly still found in southern China today, mainly in the provinces of Guizhou, Hunan, Sichuan, Guangxi and Yunnan. They can also be found in northern Vietnam and Laos.

In Thailand they are found in the following areas: Chiang Mai, Chiang Rai, Nan, Phrae, Tak, Lampang, Phayao, Phetchaburi, Phetchabun, Kamphaeng Phet, Mae Hong Son and Sukhothai.

The Meo are found in three sub-groups in Thailand:

The Blue Meo (also, confusingly, called variously the Black Meo, Flowery Meo or Striped Meo—all references to the decoration of their sometimes very colourful clothes). The women of this group wear indigo pleated skirts with batik designs;

The White Meo, whose women wear white pleated skirts for ceremonial occasions;

The Gua'mba Meo, who are mostly confined to refugee camps as they entered Thailand only during recent border disturbances in Laos.

The Meo have a patrilineal polygamous society, with strong family and clan connections operating. It is said that the Meo in Thailand have eleven clans, each of whom bears the name of people or places in ancient Meo legends.

In religion, the Meo are animists whose most powerful tribal figure is the shaman, a doctor-priest who attends to the welfare of the tribe. They are also ancestor worshippers who may well have adopted this custom from the Chinese, among whom they have lived for so long.

They prefer to live at high altitude, at least at 1,000 metres, as this is the height at which the opium poppy grows best.

They also raise other crops but are best known for the fact that their major cash crop has always been opium. Many attempts are now being made to wean them away from this.

Lahu

The Lahu are called the Musur by both the Thais and the Shan tribesmen who were their neighbours in Burma. It is thought that they came from the Tibetan hills and long ago migrated into China, Burma, Laos and, of course, Thailand.

In Thailand they can be found mainly in five provinces: Chiang Rai, Chiang Mai, Mae Hong Son, Tak and Kamphaeng Phet.

They are also divided into several groups: the Lahu Nyi, the Lahu Na, the Lahu Shehleh and the Lahu Shi. There are other sub-groups but they do not live in Thailand.

Around Chiang Mai, the easiest place to find the Lahu is off the road to Fang, on Doi Lolo, although access is somewhat difficult there. There is another more easily reached village on the Chiang Mai to Mae Suai road near Huai Muang.

Their society is patrilineal and monogamous. Often, when a man gets married, he will go to live with his wife's family for a number of years before the young couple moves out to live in a house of their own.

The Lahu are poorer than most hilltribes. They tend to wander and cultivate by the wasteful slash-and-burn method, moving on when the land is exhausted. Thus their houses are fairly primitive, and not intended for permanent shelter.

They prefer to live high up the hill slopes so as to be in closer touch with the spirits of the hills. However, this does tend to mean that they are then far away from water sources. This is obviously a problem, and leads to a general lack of sanitation and hygiene in the environment.

They grow a number of crops, including opium, and also raise a few animals for household consumption.

They are animists, though there are records of conversions to both Buddhism and Christianity, but it is still true to say that animism is the religious mainstay of the Lahu.

In tribal dress the Lahu women wear long skirts and jackets, and are often bare-breasted beneath the open jackets, while the men wear the black trousers that the Meo men wear, plus a distinguishing silver breastplate across the chest.

Yao

The Yao, or Mihn as they call themselves, came from southern China and can still be found in Guangxi and Guangdong provinces, as well as in Vietnam, Laos, Burma and Thailand.

At one time they were largely found in eastern Nan province in Thailand, but they can now also be found in the eastern parts of Chiang Rai province and around Fang in northern Chiang Mai province. They have built their houses at the roadside along the Chiang Mai to Mae Suai road.

Like other hilltribes the Yao grow opium, but only as a subsidiary crop. Their main crops are dry rice and corn.

The Yao practise polygamy, and after marriage the husband takes his wife to live with his parents. The kinship follows a patrilineal pattern. The Yao also commonly adopt children, either from within the tribe or from outside.

The Yao are at the top of the pecking order among the hilltribes. They are more open to change and are generally better educated. Since they are culturally close to the Chinese, they write in Chinese characters. They are regarded also as being the best craftsmen, and Yao embroidery is excellent and complex.

They have a written tribal history, in Chinese characters, as well as legends and the names of their ancestors. They are animists and ancestor worshippers, which they have adopted from their close relations with the Chinese.

Their tribal dress is among the most colourful of all. The women wear embroidered V-necked jackets and bright scarlet or magenta scarves rather like feather boas in appearance. They also wear large black or dark blue turbans, often embroidered. They wear loose trousers with an embroidered front panel. The men are altogether less colourful in black pyjama trousers and plain dark shirts, possibly with a narrow strip of embroidery to brighten up the front. Although many of the men now wear ordinary Thai clothes, the women still wear traditional dress even when working in the fields.

Akha

Thai people refer to the Akha as Kaw or E-kaw and they are regarded as being at the bottom of the pile in the hilltribe social order.

It is generally considered that they had their origins in the lowlands of Tibet but were forced to leave following hostilities in their homeland. They then moved to southern Yunnan province in China, and are thought to have affiliations with the Lolo tribes which lived in mainland China in ancient times.

They eventually spread across to Burma, Laos and into Thailand

probably in the 1880s, although no real records exist to confirm this.

The Akha usually live at around 1,000 metres or so. They formerly lived on the banks of the Mae Kok River, but are now moving to other places and are settled into Chiang Rai, Chiang Mai, Lampang and Phrae. Most of their settlements can be found between Chiang Mai and Chiang Rai, around Mae Suai, Mae Chan and Mae Sai.

They are monogamous and usually marry for life, living in a loosely organised patrilineal society. They do not really live in tribal form in Thailand but in extended families which form villages.

The Akha cultivate a variety of crops, none of which is opium, although a number of them are unfortunately opium addicts. As they seldom grow enough to meet their needs, they work as labourers for hire. When they travel, they often do so in the company of a pack of yapping dogs, which are choice items in the Akha diet.

In their beliefs, Akha are animists with particular interests in ancestor worship and spirit offerings. The men wear Thai clothing but the women wear decorated jackets and matching headdresses with silver coins.

Lisu

It is thought that the Lisu also originated in southern China, like so many of the other hilltribes, and about 60 years ago a number migrated into Thailand.

There are three sub-groups of Lisu: the White, or Pai, the Flowery, or Hua, and the Black, or He. Of these, only the latter two are found in Thailand.

Around Chiang Mai province can be found several settlements of Lisu —at Mae Taeng, Chiang Dao and Fang. The largest group are at Ban Khun Khong in Chiang Dao district, though there are others around Mae Hong Son and Mae Chan.

The Lisu like to live at around 1,000 metres altitude and grow a number of crops for subsistence, with opium as a cash crop.

The Lisu are divided into a number of different clans, which decide the kinship of the various groups. They are monogamous people, and marry out of the clan.

They are greatly influenced by having lived among the Chinese, and hold some of their festivals according to the Chinese calendar. Their new year is on the same day as Chinese New Year, for example. In religion they are animists.

In appearance the Lisu are taller than most of the hilltribes. The young men wear velvet coats with silver buttons and dark blue or green trousers under a frilled skirt. The women wear colourfully striped blouses and very loose trousers.

Lawa

The Lawa, who call themselves the Lavu'a, can only be found in Thailand and are thought to be the first tribe to have migrated into the hills of northern Thailand, arriving probably around AD 660. It is thought that they arrived before the Mon-Khmer and before the Thais themselves. Most of them live in the Bo Luang Plateau southwest of Chiang Mai, and the mountainous area of Umpai, southeast of Mae Hong Son. There are some Lawa villages to be seen from the road in Mae Sariang district.

They cultivate the highland areas and are very skilled at making rice terraces. Their houses are quite distinctively thatched, with a roof reaching almost down to the ground. The verandah is built under the eaves of the house instead of running along the side as in most hilltribe houses.

This is a patrilineal, monogamous society. According to anthropologists, the society is divided into two sections. The greater number of people are Lua, or common people, while the rest are the descendants of the great Lua king, Khun Luang Wilanka. His descendants are called Kun.

In religion, the Lawa are animists and Buddhists, usually combining the two satisfactorily.

The Lawa do not have the somewhat Chinese appearance of many of the hilltribes. Instead they look more like North American Indians. The men dress all in white, while a married woman wears a long, dark-blue dress tied at the waist. Unmarried women wear the same thing, but in white.

Khamu

The Khamu have come over from various parts of Laos, mainly to find work in the teak forests of Thailand, and a number of them have since settled in Thailand.

They live mainly in Nan, Lampang and Kanchanaburi. They are found in small villages on the mountain slopes where they subsist on agriculture, hunting, fishing and trading.

The Khamu are animists, and in Laos they are greatly respected for their ability as shamans.

H'tin

Unless you are in Nan province, you are unlikely to come across any H'tin, a small tribe who apparently migrated into Thailand only in the last 40 to 80 years.

They live in houses built on piles, with bamboo floors and walls.

They are monogamous. After marriage the husband will move in with his wife's parents for several years—typical of matrilineal societies such as this.

Usually the H'tin are animists, unless they have converted to Buddhism, which is not unknown.

Mrabri

The Mrabri, or Yumbri, are known to the Thais as the Phi Tong Luang, which means the 'spirits of the yellow leaves'. There are only about 70 members of this threatened tribe left, living in Nan province.

They are highly nomadic, moving every three or four days, and live by hunting and gathering. Sometimes they work for the Meo and the H'tin, but they never own their own rice fields.

They are patrilineal and go about in groups of three to twelve individuals. It is most unlikely that the average visitor will ever see any of this tiny tribe.

South of Chiang Mai

Nan

Nan is actually to the east, but as it has special attractions it is well worth trekking across to see. Nan itself is a fairly nondescript country town, with the usual rather empty activity that characterises so many little Thai towns. But the countryside surrounding Nan is beautiful—lush, green, quiet, hilly. The town is old, dating from the 15th century, but it has been rebuilt and changed since then. Nevertheless there are several old temples to see—for example, **Wat Phumin,** built in 1496 and restored in 1867 in Sukhothai style.

The most famous aspect of Nan is that every year at the end of the rainy season the town holds boat races very similar to the **Dragon Boat** races held by Chinese communities throughout Southeast Asia. It is a colourful and camera-worthy occasion.

Lamphun

This is an individualistic little town only 26 kilometres from Chiang Mai which was once an independent though tiny capital under a Mon princess, and still retains its separateness. It is set in rich countryside and is surrounded by protective walls and a moat. As you enter the town you will pass the **Wat Phra That Haripunchai.** This temple is named after the ancient kingdom of which Lamphun was the capital back in the 9th century. The temple is an odd mixture of everything from the very ancient to the modern, since each age seems to have added a little more to the complex. You can find every style known to Thai history here—a Dvaravati-style *chedi,* a Chiang Saen-style *chedi,* Sukhothai-style images, right up to a sanctuary built in 1925.

Another scramble of styles can be seen in the **Wat Ku Kut,** also known as the Wat Cham Thewi. This lies just over the city moat on the left and is also interesting to look over.

The other two delights of Lamphun are its woven cloth and the beauty of its women — both of which you will find ample examples of as you stroll around this quiet little backwater of history.

Lampang

Lampang lies at the junction of the roads from Chiang Mai and Chiang Rai and is one of the few Thai towns which has not been overwhelmed in the worst possible way by modern development. It still retains the old-style tiled-roof houses of the Chinese merchants, and it is the only town in the whole of Thailand which still uses the small horse-drawn carriages which were once a popular form of transport for those who could afford to ride. The main part of the old city lies in quiet sheltered garden quarters on the edge of the Mae Nam Wang River. There are a number of excellent temples to visit, including a number of Burmese-style temples and shrines. Lampang is thought by historians to have been the capital of a Mon kingdom before the Khmers arrived on the scene, let alone the later-arriving Thais.

The **Wat Phra Kaeo** is where the Emerald Buddha, now in Bangkok in the Temple of the Emerald Buddha, was once kept. If you want to see the best temple in this area, however, you must drive 16 kilometres south to **Wat Phra That Lampang Luang,** which is massive and very much revered as a shrine. It even has its own Emerald Buddha, a small carved image which legend says came from the identical block from which the famous Emerald Buddha was carved. It is a very extensive complex and contains many sacred images, including one dating from 1476. Its many treasures and its isolated rural setting make it well worth your attention.

Sukhothai

Whether you regard Sukhothai as north of Bangkok or south of Chiang Mai, it is quite far from either. It lies 450 kilometres from Bangkok, and it is here that the first capital city of the Thai nation was established and grew to its zenith during the period 1257 to 1389.

The flowering of this city was very much connected with the flowering of the southern school of Buddhism — Theravada or Hinayana Buddhism — which was imported from Sri Lanka. As in Sri Lanka, the coming of Buddhism seems to have been the making of a splendid city, in which the temples and palaces were themselves tribute to the wisdom of Buddha. The particular style of architecture typified as Sukhothai style, towering, elaborately-decorated structures with a very stylised approach, is in marked contrast to the more individualistic Khmer style.

There is a lot to see, and it is essential to allow plenty of time and a good pair of comfortable shoes. The city is spread out, because it was built on the spacious lines of other great Buddhist cities — such as the 50-mile wide holy

city of Anuradhapura in Sri Lanka—and it will be meaningless unless you allow yourself time to absorb what a huge achievement this was. It is now a scattering of many ruined and half-ruined remains, and you must take time to let your mind piece it all together. Quick tours—though they are the norm—are frankly a waste of time.

Forget about going to the more remote parts of Sukhothai, beyond the city towards the hills. It is not safe at the moment, as there are too many bandits running around and queueing up to rob you. Check it out, though, as the situation could change. Ask around, and if people warn you off, take their advice.

The easiest way to tackle the task of Sukhothai is to think of the city in five sections—the walled city and the museum, then north, south, east and west.

The walled city and museum includes the imposing ruins of **Wat Mahathat**. This is the biggest in a big city. It is centred on a towering *chedi* and boasts some impressively restored standing Buddhas and seated figures. It is considered to be a particularly good example of the Sukhothai decoration motif—the lotus bud.

The **Museum** will give you a sense of orientation. It has excellent scale models of the city, and you can buy a good little guidebook.

Wat Si Sawai, just south of Mahathat, is a well-preserved Khmer-style Hindu sanctuary, complete with three pagodas decorated with the original stucco. This dates from the 12th century, just before the founding of the kingdom of Sukhothai.

Wat Sra Si, to the north, is a ruin still in excellent enough shape to be pretty impressive—six rows of columns on a platform with a well-restored seated Buddha. This is a beautifully harmonised temple in design, detail and setting.

Wat Phra Pai Luang, also north, is another temple pre-dating the Sukhothai period. It has a fine *chedi* and is surrounded by seated Buddhas which were hidden for many years and only found during restoration, walled up behind the stucco. It also has three Khmer-style towers. This temple is thought to have been the centre of the Khmer city which occupied the site before it became the Sukhothai capital.

Wat Si Chum is still used for worship and houses a colossal restored standing Buddha. The narrow passageway leading to this is covered with drawings which can only be seen by torch or candlelight, so dark is the windowless corridor.

Wat Trapang Thong Lang, to the east, is a small sanctuary set round by columns and noted for the stucco decoration on the walls of the chapel. The panel on the southern side is often photographed.

Wat Chedi Sung is all that remains of a temple which must have once dominated the whole countryside. The *chedi* is considered to be the finest example of Sukhothai architecture still extant.

Getting around the ruins of Sukhothai takes an awful lot of walking. So it would be sensible to hire either a bicycle or, for the lazier, a *tuktuk* at an hourly rate which can vary considerably from 20 baht up to 50 baht. Bargain hard and try to get one in the modern city, where it is cheaper. Once you are already at the ruins, the price is much higher.

Phitsanulok

Called Phit for short, Phitsanulok has only one thing worth seeing and that is the Jinaraj Buddha in the **Wat Phra Si Ratana.** This is Thailand's most revered and most copied image. Otherwise, apart from being a reasonably agreeable little town, there is no other reason why you should get off the train.

The South

There is a different country down South—long empty beaches of fine sand, palm trees, tropical fruit and all the delights of the sea. It is one whole area of Thailand where the simple beachside life of Robinson Crusoe is more than possible, plus of course a few comforts which Crusoe had to forgo but which, as a visitor, you can enjoy—good food and elegantly simple accommodation.

Not only is it geographically different along the southern peninsula, culturally it is another place altogether. This is not Thai Thailand, of Buddha shrines and hilltribes. This is Muslim, almost-Malay Thailand, where people largely live off the fruit of the sea which dominates their lives.

It is very beautiful and, for those who yearn for the unspoiled, has scarcely been touched by tourism. How long this will remain true is in question, so perhaps this is the best time to go there. Phuket is already well developed—or over-developed, according to your feelings about these things—and the Thai government has ambitious plans for the innocent tropical island of Ko Samui—so hurry.

There are many small and delightful islands scattered around the whole southern peninsula. There are national parks and conservation areas full of sea life, turtles, birds and exotic small mammals, where you can stay overnight in simple and adequate accommodation at a modest cost. There are tiny fishing villages where you can rent a beach bungalow and drink in sunshine and dine on lobsters and fresh seafood caught by the villagers. There are the so-called sea gypsies, colourful sea-going folk who may well have more connections than they should with the notorious pirates of the Gulf of Thailand.

Food is different too—more the Malay style of cuisine, with liberal use of coconut milk to cool those fierce Thai curries—and the further south you go the more likely you are to hear Malay spoken. In fact in recent times this area was independent, ruled over by a number of local sultans, and it has only been in the 20th century that it has really been integrated into the kingdom of Thailand. There is still some way to go in terms of integration, and there are those who resist the attempts of the Thai government to bring about an even fuller integration. Consequently the development and improvement of conditions in the South has been an important part of Thai policy of the last few years, and the Royal Family has established near the southern border at Narathiwat a palace which is now on their regular schedule of visits.

This is a very rich region of Thailand, agriculturally and aquatically, and therefore commercial development is moving fairly swiftly ahead, with more tourist-oriented plans being laid for the border area. The great majority of tourists in the South come over the border from Malaysia, but there is no doubt that as more tourists become aware of the great delights of the southern peninsula a larger number of overseas visitors will head for places other than Phuket.

There are many buses and trains from Bangkok down the peninsula, although you can also go by boat and, of course, there are daily flights from Bangkok airport and other parts of Thailand. In this section we follow the main routes south from Bangkok, highlighting those attractions of the greatest interest to tourists.

Hua Hin

This favourite Thai seaside resort, only 227 kilometres from Bangkok, is where Bangkok Thais like to head for a quiet seaside weekend. Not really promoted by the TAT, it has a quiet charm of its own and, because it has not been touched by the more brash aspects of tourism, will delight those who seek something off the beaten track without having to suffer any discomforts.

The Thai Royal Family has a splendid holiday villa here where it usually spends some of the hottest season of the year. There is an excellent beach, with fine white sand, and good swimming except for big wave days. Don't take risks.

Most people like to stay at the Railway Hotel. The name may not be very romantic, but it is a dignified old colonial-style structure with personality. The high season for Hua Hin are the months from March to May, when all the restaurants are fully operative and the weather pleasant.

Further south from Hua Hin, just beyond the town of **Pran Buri,** is **Khao Sam Roi Yot National Park.** The name means 'mountain of 300 peaks', and you'll begin to see why from the road. The park consists of 130 square kilometres of dramatic limestone hills, densely forested slopes and valleys, waterfalls, boat rides, quiet beaches and an awful lot of wildlife.

Among the more notable animal and bird residents of the park are the rare herds of serow, an animal which is a cross between a goat and a deer, macaques and langurs, Irrawady dolphins along the coastal part of the park, porcupines, leopards and barking deer. Birds include 27 varieties of wader, painted storks, egrets, grey herons and many other marsh birds.

There are some splendid caves, a favourite being the **Phraya Nakhon Cave.** It was discovered about 200 years ago by the ruler of the same name, who was washed ashore during a severe storm and found the cave by accident. There is a royal pavilion inside the cave, built for King Rama V's visit in 1896 and still occasionally in use.

Visitors can explore secluded nature trails, spend time on the beaches, arrange boat trips with local fishermen and enjoy watching the regular appearances of schools of dolphins which inhabit the sea in this area.

They can also stay in the park accommodation—three bungalows and four campgrounds. But be warned: savage mosquitoes reside here, so take a good repellent with you.

Chaiya

Chaiya, further south near Surat Thani, is considered to have been the site of an ancient and refined culture, but historians and archaeologists do not agree which it was. Some consider this to have been the site of an ancient city which was the capital of the Srivichai kingdom, while others claim that the Indonesian style of the statues found in Chaiya indicate that it was the capital of a province of a kingdom based in Sumatra.

The **Wat Phra Boromathat,** a temple on the road before the town, is the most important monument left of that ancient kingdom. It has been excavated and partially restored and boasts three large sandstone Buddhas and a cloister gallery which shelters many Buddha statues in striking Javanese style.

In the little museum nearby you can see some copies of the most impressive of the statues and images found here and transported to the National Museum in Bangkok. The buildings are open from 9am to noon and 1pm to 4pm, closed on Mondays and Tuesdays.

There are other ruins quite near—a brick *chedi* at **Wat Long,** the portico of **Wat Ratanaram** and some Srivichai remains at **Wat Keo,** also restored. Each has some hints of the glory now lost.

An unusual attraction in Chaiya is the **Wat Suan Mok,** a modern temple filled with an amazing collection of paintings on all kinds of subjects—not only Buddhist—done by a wandering Zen disciple, American Emmanuel Sherman. This is a forest wat, some 60 hectares of trees and hills which offers spiritual shelter to monks and other seekers, but in its idiosyncratic way far from orthodox. Worth a visit out of pure interest, let alone for its peaceful and contemplative air.

Surat Thani

Surat Thani comes next, 651 kilometres from Bangkok. It is a busy commercial centre, of little interest except to those heading for the tropical paradise of Ko Samui. It has more or less merged with the neighbouring sprawl of **Ban Don.** It is fine to wander around in and has a good market, but there really is not a lot to attract the tourist unless he happens to be there anyway. Most people do not consider it worth staying overnight in these towns.

Ko Samui

This island is Thailand's answer to Bali, and many travellers think it gives that legendary isle a good run for its money. It is an open secret among the knowledgeable that this is the place to go if you love good beaches, swimming and snorkelling, nature, living beside the beach or even on it and having a great and unspoiled time.

It is one of a group of some eighty islands, big and small, and it is about 250 square kilometres in area. It is covered with coconut plantations and divided by a mountain ridge. Samui is the biggest island of the group. The other two islands mainly visited by tourists are **Ko Phangan** and **Ko Tao.**

There are said to be 35,000 people on Samui, largely depending upon the sea for their livelihood, with some additional income from the coconut-based agriculture. The island is extraordinarily pretty—villages nestle beside little rocky coves, waterfalls thread their way down the cliffs and the houses of the villagers are sheltered by the coconut palms.

There is a road which runs round the island, though it is not a good one. For the transport-minded, you can hire motorbikes for 150 baht a day or bicycles for about 30 baht per half day and 50 baht per day, and these are available throughout the island from anywhere you care to stop. You can also hire boats for the various trips out from Ko Samui or, if you're really that energetic, for rowing around. Bargain hard for them.

When you arrive on Ko Samui, you will undoubtedly arrive at **Ban Ang Thong.** There are a variety of ways to arrive but they all end up on ferries. Most people come from Surat Thani by bus and then take the ferry. The ferry leaves from the little port of Ban Don at noon and midnight, taking about six hours for the trip. There is, however, also a speedboat which leaves at noon and takes only three hours. The State Railway, at the time of writing, was offering a special train-bus-boat combination out of Bangkok at reasonable rates. Check it out for yourself.

Once on Ko Samui, there are two ways to get around the whole island— apart from hiring personal transport. Go by the taxi trucks which run everywhere and cost a nominal sum only (unless you hire the whole truck, in which case you bargain for a price) or hire a boat and sail around the

Thai classical dancers

coast. As for accommodation, there are many places to stay—all much the same in their simplicity with just slight variations on standards. Stop wherever you like the look of the beach and book a bungalow or room there. If you don't like it, get up and move on, since there is no problem about finding alternative places.

As soon as you get off the ferry, you will be besieged by touts offering you bungalows, bungalows and more bungalows. There is also one hotel on the island, and a resort—so you can pick your price level. It would be a good idea to know roughly what you want and where, in order to deal with this little furore. As a guide, all the beaches are lovely but the northern beaches are even quieter and less developed than the rest. There are minibuses waiting for every ferry—at the time of writing it was 15 baht to go north, and 10-15 baht for Lamai and Chawang beaches where the majority of travellers stay. Of these two, Lamai is the quietest.

Be warned: everything costs more on Ko Samui, as all goods have to be brought from the mainland. So be sure you already have your film, torches, batteries, candles, mosquito repellent, suntan lotion and all the rest before you get on that ferry boat. You'll be sorry when you have to pay as much as double on the island.

As a further guide, most bungalows in early 1984 cost about 30 baht a day, which is a good price. It is possible that further tourism development may change this. Food is already expensive, at 30 baht plus for meals. Also, if you are attracted by the thought of those peaceful northern beaches, you should know that all electricity comes from generators and there are unlikely to be any fittings for your electric shaver. Also, all the ice comes from town. So when we use the word simple, we mean it!

There are two waterfalls worth a trip—the **Hin Lad Waterfall,** only a few kilometres from the port and walkable all the way, and the **Na Muang Waterfall** in the centre of the island, about ten kilometres from the port. Take a taxi truck if you don't fancy the exercise and pay around 10 baht. You can also visit the Na Muang Waterfall from Lamai and Chawang beaches.

When all this sea, sunshine and nature gets to be a little much, there are also temples worth visiting. The **Wat Na Phra Lan,** the main *chedi* of which is said to contain the bones of a revered holy man, Kru Pudson, who legend says could cure diseases miraculously and calm a raging sea, and at the northern end of the island the temple of the Big Buddha, reached by a causeway. This is a modern image about twelve metres high and it looks good in silhouette against the tropical sunset. This is actually a meditation centre for monks. When they are in residence, which is only an occasional event, they enjoy having visitors. As this semi-island is enclosed by a large sheltering bay, the waters can be rather murky, presumably due to less water movement, but it is very quiet and peaceful.

Lamai Beach is very popular among those who seek a natural life and plenty of fun—good food and video movies in the evenings. The beach is long and clean and the waters are clear. The north end is quieter and has a good selection of bungalows, costing more than elsewhere but good value (up to 80 baht). You can find cheaper, but you get less, so choose accordingly. There are plenty of taxis back to town when the simple life palls.

Nude bathing abounds, though the authorities frown on it, and for the eager reader there is a library of English, French and German books at the Magic Bungalow which you can rent for 10 baht per week.

This was really a little fishing village before young travellers started coming to Ko Samui, and the villagers still continue their own lives amid all the modern misbehaviour. They live in their own Thai-style houses, catch fish and sell them to the tourists.

Chawang Beach is bigger, more developed and busier, but it is far from being Bangkok. The beach is twice as big as Lamai, and opposite the tiny island of Mat Lang. It does not, however, have the coral garden that Lamai does, but still offers good swimming in clear waters.

There is another beach at **Bophut,** but the water is rather dirty-looking and it really is not so attractive.

Next to Ko Samui is another island well worth visiting, **Ko Phangan.** It is a half-hour sea journey away and the ferry costs 25 baht. As the water

around Ko Phangan is too shallow for the ferry, small fishing boats come out to take people in to shore. There again, visitors are met by hordes of eager bungalow owners touting for custom. They will take you to their bungalow, which is convenient as there are only three minibuses on the island. When you want to travel further, you will probably use a motorcycle. Don't be surprised to find yourself sharing it with at least one other passenger, and don't worry too much—the Thais are used to that kind of thing. Very cheap way to travel.

Ko Phangan is for those who think that even Ko Samui is not far enough away from modern life. It is said to be about five years behind it in development. It has dirt roads, tiny villages with superbly friendly people in them, and once again those legendary beaches. The best beaches are on the southeastern tip of the island. There is a road but it goes only as far as Ban Kai where, at low tide, you can walk to the beach. If the tide is in, you must hire a fishing boat to take you the four kilometres to the best place to stay, **Hardrint.**

Hardrint Beach is a favourite—long, with fine sand, clear blue waters and a good selection of bungalows. In the rainy season it can be windy down here. You can wander, with difficulty, to other neighbouring beaches past the coconut palms and into desert isle territory. Do not take any risks around here, as some of the rocky paths can be dangerous and you could fall. Follow the established tracks and do not be foolishly adventurous. If you want to go further north, hire a fishing boat to take you to the even more sheltered coves round the coast.

The loveliest place to stay is reasonably near Ban Kai, where the three bungalows are sheltered and have superb views of the nearby islands and the sunsets. Only about 20 to 30 baht. For the spiritual, there is a Vipasana meditation centre high up on a mountain in the centre of the island where you can stay and think about the transience of all the beauty around you. Or, if you are still interested in the holy but don't want to do it yourself, visit **Wat Bodhi** near Ban Kai. There is a very friendly monk there who likes to take tea with visitors and practise his English on them.

When you want to return to Ko Samui—if you ever do—the return ferry leaves at 6am each morning and starts loading at 5.30am. It would probably be a good idea to stay in the village overnight if you have to make this boat.

A third island which attracts many visitors is **Ko Tao,** or Turtle Island. It is a four-hour trip from Samui, so it will take a full day to go both ways. The fishing boat will take you to a small village called Ao Mae Hat, where you will find restaurants, village houses and all the lovely paraphernalia of local life—fishing nets, coconut palms, wandering animals and fish salting. Wander away around the island and you will find empty beaches and sheltered coves where you can bathe and sun yourself all day and not see another soul. The island is also famed for papayas.

Other little islands in the group of eighty are the source of the famous bird's nest of soup fame. These are the nests of sea swallows, made from solidified saliva which is much appreciated by the Chinese. Best quality comes from the first harvest nests, and collecting them from narrow ledges high above the pounding sea is a risky business indeed.

When planning your trip to the Ko Samui group of islands, remember to check on boat times, since they change frequently and there is a tendency for times to be rather loosely adhered to.

The best time of the year for visiting them is during the dry season from February to June. The rainy season spoils your sunbathing plans from July to October, and from October to January there can be altogether too much wind for comfort.

Nakhon Si Thammarat

This southern town, 814 kilometres from Bangkok, is usually called Nakhon for short. Under another name, Ligor, it was once a very important site in history. There is a great deal of argument as to what exactly that history was, but it is agreed that the town was one of the oldest sites in Thailand.

Some historians say that this was the centre of the Srivichai Empire, while others say that it was the capital of a dependency of the rulers who made their capital in Palembang in Sumatra. This is also where the Thai shadow puppet drama and the classical dance-drama developed, and where Thai nielloware was first made.

It is set in glorious countryside, and the drive to the town takes you through beautiful winding valleys, past distant hills and into the rice paddies.

There are some things worth visiting in the town too. It has a pleasant dignity conferred on it by the historical monuments around, and has the nickname Muang Phra, which means holy city. The town is split by a clock tower, and most of the things you want to see are south of the market.

The best is **Wat Mahathat,** one of the oldest temples in Thailand, with a courtyard in which stands a 77-metre high *chedi,* the top of which is covered with gold leaf and encrusted with precious stones. The chapels are covered with paintings and hold many sacred images. There is also a small museum packed full of precious objects—gold and silver pieces made by the best of local craftsmen, Chinese porcelain and Sukhothai ceramics, as well as two beautiful images—a standing stone Buddha of the Dvaravati period and a seated Buddha in Srivichai style.

Right next door is the **Viharn Luang,** a highly decorated building with pillars which lean inwards, an Ayutthaya structure.

The town also boasts an excellent small museum, a two-storey building with antiquities from the whole region, showing its rich cultural heritage with Indian and Thai figures and artefacts.

When you tire of monuments, walk around the streets and observe the craftsmen at work—gold and silversmiths and puppet-makers making the dried leather figures which feature in shadow plays. You may also be tempted to buy the handsome nielloware—it looks like enamel but it is actually a black alloy which fills the spaces between lines of gold or silver, rather like a form of cloisonne.

It is always being predicted that Nakhon is about to be discovered, routed to the main southern highways and then turned into a tourist trap. So far this has not yet happened, so get there soon.

Songkhla

Songkhla is quietly left meditating upon its colourful history in pleasantly unspoiled settings, while other towns roar ahead into unattractive modernity. This was once a largely Chinese city, an important seaport for the Dutch in the spice war days of Asia when Europeans first battled their way into the rich continent.

Formerly known as Singora, Songkhla guards the way to the Talay Sap, Thailand's largest lake, and offers a safe harbour for the numerous fishing boats of the South. The town itself is still a racial mixing pot—Thais, Malays, Chinese and Indians live contentedly in this port which has become, literally, a backwater. Large vessels cannot get into Songkhla. They have to anchor outside between the shore and two islands nicely named Ko Maeo and Ko Nu, or Cat and Mouse islands. There is a long white beach—though if you have just come from Ko Samui you may not be so impressed—and a harmonious blend of old and new around the town. The beach is lined with casuarina trees and there are many good places to eat opposite the beach.

There is a colourful waterfront area, full of the bustle and activity that typifies such districts, and there are also 314 Buddhist temples and 185 mosques in the town, of which, it must be said, very few are outstanding in a way which attracts visitors. However the **Wat Klang,** also known as **Wat Yak,** is the central temple and has charm enough to make it worth a visit. It has some paintings in a building called the Sala Russi which show hermits doing yoga exercises, and some notable frescoes inside done about a hundred years ago by a Bangkok artist. They show daily life as it was lived then, and shine with vitality.

The **Talay Sap,** often called Songkhla Lake, has something for most tastes—fishing, boating, picnic excursions to the many tree-covered islands which dot the surface of the lake. The best of these is Yor, at the southern end of the lake. Make a deal with a boatman to get there.

If you want to go to a specific place you could take a water taxi for a small sum, but you will need to be up and about at around 7am. If you want to have your own boat for the entire day, which will allow you to explore the whole lake, don't expect much change out of 100 baht. On Ko Yor you can find people involved in the cottage industry of homespun cotton, producing good ethnic patterns, available at reasonable prices—if you bargain hard.

Hat Yai

This town is 1,289 kilometres from Bangkok, and is an important commercial and communications centre. Its name means 'large beach' but there is, alas, no beach to be seen there any more. There are shops, though, and that is one of the main features of Hat Yai, since it has become a virtual shopping centre for Malaysians who like to come across the border to do their duty-free shopping. Most of the shops are run by Chinese.

Seventy years ago there was nothing where Hat Yai now is. Then it became a little village, turning into an important town—one of the biggest in Thailand—with the construction of the railway line from Bangkok to Malaysia during the reign of King Rama VI. It is not a town with much character, and it has few attractions.

There is the **Hat Yai Municipal Park,** a level plain surrounded by small hills. There is a lake and pleasant enough greenery around to make a quiet stroll worth taking.

The **Rubber Research Centre** was actually established for rubber experts from throughout Thailand, but you can see demonstrations of rubber tapping there if you want to.

The **Hat Yai Nai Temple** is what most tourists go for—a 35-metre long reclining Buddha in a temple just west of town, four kilometres from the river bridge of Hat Yai. The Buddha, called the Phra Puttahat Mongkol Buddha, is being restored, as is the temple itself.

About 20 kilometres from town is the **Ton Nga Chang Waterfall.** The name means 'elephant tusk waterfall', so-called because of the shape of the rock formation over which the water flows. The track approaching the falls is quite rough and the actual waterfall, which is split into two levels, is one of the most impressive in the South.

If you want beaches, get on the bus for Songkhla, which is only about 30 kilometres away.

One of the attractions of Hat Yai—apart from all the stereo shops—is **bull-fighting.** This is not at all like Spanish bull-fighting. In Thailand the fight is between two bulls, and fortunately it is not a fight to the death, only to capitulation by one of the contestants. Drums signal the start of the day's contests, which continue all day from 10.30am until early evening. The first and second weekend of every month are the days, and admission varies from 10 to 30 baht. **Thai boxing** contests are held at the Television Stadium every Saturday from 2pm to 5pm, admission five baht.

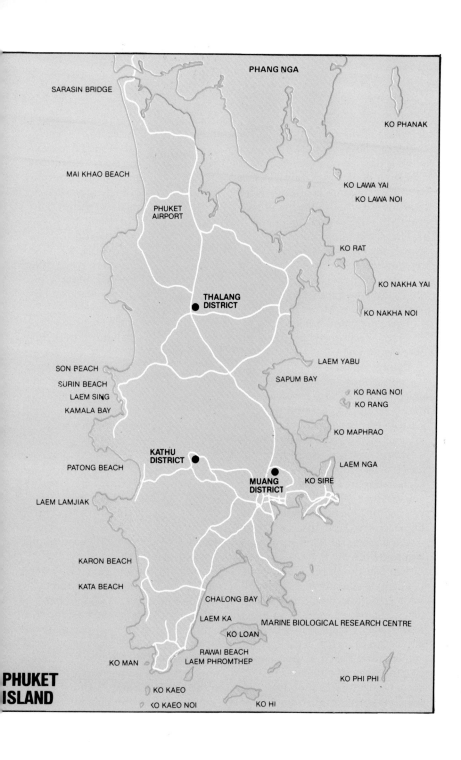

PHANG NGA

SARASIN BRIDGE

KO PHANAK

MAI KHAO BEACH

KO LAWA YAI
KO LAWA NOI

PHUKET
AIRPORT

KO RAT

KO NAKHA YAI

THALANG
DISTRICT

KO NAKHA NOI

LAEM YABU

SON BEACH
SURIN BEACH
LAEM SING
KAMALA BAY

SAPUM BAY

KO RANG NOI
KO RANG

KO MAPHRAO

KATHU
DISTRICT

LAEM NGA

PATONG BEACH

MUANG
DISTRICT

KO SIRE

LAEM LAMJIAK

KARON BEACH

KATA BEACH

CHALONG BAY

LAEM KA

MARINE BIOLOGICAL RESEARCH CENTRE

KO LOAN

KO MAN

RAWAI BEACH
LAEM PHROMTHEP

**PHUKET
ISLAND**

KO PHI PHI

KO KAEO
KO KAEO NOI

KO HI

Phuket

The Pearl of the South, according to the tourist brochures, and perhaps deserving of the name. Phuket is an island province, the centre of a whole cluster of islands set in the emerald green splendour of the Andaman Sea, and it is now being promoted in a big way as the tropical island paradise of Thailand. Well, it is certainly not as unspoiled as Ko Samui, but it does have many charms. It offers beach life at any level, from highest class de luxe down to the simple life in rattan and bamboo bungalows within sight and sound of the sea.

The island has beaches, palm trees, mountains, snorkelling and swimming, good food and plenty of trips out and about. It really is excellent for families or individual travellers. In culture Phuket—like other southern centres—has a mixed Thai, Chinese and Malay style about it, plus the visiting sea gypsies, the colourful seafarers—and pirates—who can be seen anchored together in sheltered little coves.

There are many beaches to choose from and you could well go to a different beach every day for a week and find them all delightful in their different ways.

Patong Beach is said to be the finest, but this depends upon your tastes. It is also among the most developed, and some people might prefer a quieter, more private beach to themselves. This long curving beach is found about 15 kilometres out of town along the Wichit Songkram Road. It is edged by casuarina trees and palms and there are bungalows for hire, some of them expensive by Thai standards.

Rawai Beach is where you can find the sea gypsies, known as *orang rawot*. This is another sheltered bay, usually with some fishing boats anchored in it. There are a number of tiny rocky islets around here, and you can hire fishing boats to take you there. This is a shell haven too, and you can find accommodation at all price levels. Follow the south road for 16 kilometres to get there.

Ao Karon and **Ao Kata** are west-facing beaches, only really good in mild weather. Both are favourites among low-budget travellers.

Hat Nai Beach lies south, and is separated from Patong Beach by several bays and headlands, with a beautiful coastal road leading to it. At the 13-kilometre stone, take the first track to the right, then the right hand fork where the path divides. You pass through rice paddies on the way and the beach itself is sheltered by trees. It is small, private and very peaceful. It is also cheap to stay in, with very limited local accommodation.

Nai Yang Beach is another secluded spot, good for swimming and edged by pine trees. It is mostly Thais who come here, and there is very little accommodation for rent. It fronts on to the **Hat Nai Yang National Park,** which is both a land and sea conservation area. The boundary extends into the Andaman Sea and protects the largely undisturbed coral reefs and the

sea turtles which nest on the beach. It is one of the few areas of Thailand where the leatherneck turtles lay eggs. The beach is fine white sand kept very clean, and it's quieter than other beaches around Phuket. Being near the airport, it is not surprisingly also known as Airport Beach. You can hire a glass-bottomed boat to see the extensive coral gardens, or at low tide walk out and snorkel. There are some bungalows for hire, a camping ground and some restaurants. A small number of snorkels can be hired.

This area is about 32 kilometres from town along the airport road. A few kilometres further north is the longest beach on Phuket, the **Mai Khao Beach,** where sea turtles lay their eggs from November to February.

Surin Beach is about 24 kilometres from town. It is a nice-looking stretch of sand but has a treacherous sea with strong undercurrents. It is not really very safe to swim here. However, you can play golf on the course just inland from the beachfront. Just south of here is yet another beach, the very beautiful small beach of **Laem Sing** with its odd rock formations. One more kilometre south again and you find **Kamala Bay** by following the cliff path which snakes along the hillsides. The northern part of the beach is good for swimming but the south is stony.

If you get tired of beach-crawling, then there are the many islands which surround the main island of Phuket. Try **Ko Sire,** a small island to the southeast cut off by the Tha Chin Canal. There is a religious retreat here, and a large reclining Buddha dominates the hilltop in the centre of the island, but there is nothing very remarkable to see. Of more interest is the sea people's village further on where everyone shares the same surname. They are a separate race from the Thais, and are divided into those who are still seagoing and those who live solely on land. They have their own language, culture and religious beliefs, and experts think they probably came originally from the Andaman and Nicobar islands. It does not cost much to hire a boat to go to this island, and others around, but you should go in a group. On an individual basis, it does cost. You could also pick up a local tour organised by travel agents on Phuket.

Ko Kaeo Phitsadan, or **Ko Kaeo Yai,** is a tiny isle just one kilometre off Rawai Beach. Here there are scenic and coral-laden seas, plus a holy footprint revered by local people as the Buddha's footprint.

Wat Phra Thong, near Thalang district town, is a curious monument where a half-buried Buddha image is the focal point. Legend says that this used to be pasture, and that once a young boy tied his water buffalo to the half-buried column in the field. Soon both the boy and his charge became sick, and it was then found that the column was the decorative top of a Buddha image. The villagers tried to dig up the image in order to erect it as a shrine, but they could only manage to expose the top half. When the Burmese invaded Thalang they also tried to dig up the column, but were driven off by a swarm of hornets. The villagers then built a shelter over the half-buried image, and that is what remains today.

Limestone wonders in Phang Nga Bay

Another waterfall worth seeing is to be found in the **Ton Sai Waterfall National Park,** about 20 kilometres from town along the Thep Kasittri Road to Thalang district, then right for three kilometres and you find yourself in the expansive greenery of the park.

The town of Phuket itself is not worth much more than friendly attention. There are some good markets at which you can buy cotton goods, craftwork and all kinds of food and drink.

Most people do not leave Phuket without going to **Phang Nga Bay,** some 75 kilometres from Phuket town along the Thep Kasittri Road, across the Sarasin Bridge and on to Khok Kloi. Take the signposted road to Surakun Pier or continue to a second signpost and take the path to Custom Pier. Hire boats and take the tour which goes all around the bay. The bay is surrounded by sheer mountains, rugged little islands and limestone rocks jutting right out of the sea itself. Some of the rocks scattered in the bay soar to over 300 metres high, and arching cave mouths hung with stalactites and stalagmites gape out over the green and peaceful waters of the bay. It would be best to stay for several days in the area if you can, even though the range of accommodation available is not good. Many take a half-day tour quickly round the most accessible parts of the bay. A pity—it is this bay which appears on so many of the Phuket posters you see in travel agencies.

Suwankhuha Caves, past the 30-kilometre mark at Takua Thung, have a number of Buddha images in them, situated among the striking collection of stalagmites and stalactites.

Try also the amusingly named **Phi Phi Islands,** of which there are two, the flat Phi Phi Don and the rocky cliff-edged Phi Phi Le. They have caves inhabited by swallows, and clear seas through which you can see a wealth of marine life. Get there by boat from Rawai Beach.

The shell graveyards of **Susan Hoi** are worth the trip from Khok Kloi along past Phang Nga Bay. Here you can see the accumulation of millions of years of tidal deposits, a vast graveyard of shells laid by a trick of the ocean.

National Parks

Thailand has a strong policy on conservation, and has set aside some 25,000 square kilometres of countryside to form the basis of the 42 national parks which offer rare opportunities to the visitor to get deep into unspoiled land rich in wildlife. Another four national parks will soon be joining this total.

The first park set up was the Khao Yai National Park, set up in the Northeast in 1962, and now the parks cover all kinds of terrain—soaring mountains, tropical forests, languid coastlines and the pick of Thailand's wildlife. The most recent figures indicate that almost three million visitors a year explore the national parks, but in the overall picture of tourism this still means that only a fraction of those who go to Thailand take the opportunity to investigate this rich heritage of nature.

As there are 42 parks, this chapter will cover only the largest and most obviously interesting. However, for those with a keen interest in really getting into this rather under-explored aspect of Thailand, the Shell Company of Thailand has published an excellent guide to at least 23 of the parks. This guide is obtainable from the Shell Company of Thailand Limited, P.O. Box 345, Bangkok, Thailand at a cost of 100 baht, and is well worth getting if wildlife is your thing. You can also buy it in most bookshops in Thailand.

Doi Inthanon National Park

This park is best reached from Chiang Mai along the Chom Thong road. It is possible both to walk and to drive in Doi Inthanon, and which you do depends upon your energy and the time available. The motor road follows the walking trail anyway. There are a number of Karen and Meo villages along the way, since most of these hilltribes people were already living in the park before it became so designated.

The first part of the ascent towards Thailand's highest peak is through beautiful forest, but this gives way to lush grassy slopes and hills as you get

Meo village on Doi Inthanon

nearer the peak. About nine kilometres from the summit you enter an
enclosed military area and pass a road check. From this point onwards you
may be enclosed in mist at any point. The vegetation becomes tropical
mountaintop forest, with trees and rocks covered with damp moss. You will
need a sweater for this stretch, as the mist will chill you. If you are driving,
be careful where you stop your vehicle, as a hill-start is no joke at 8,500 feet
and may in fact be impossible. As well as evergreens, you will find orchids,
sphagnum moss and everlasting roses during the winter season.

This used to be an area rich in the larger mammals—tiger, clouded
leopard, bear—but the activities of another mammal, man, have now
ruined that. However, you may catch glimpses of white-handed gibbons
around the lower slopes, the Assamese macaque and the Phayre's langur.
Near the peak live Thailand's only species of two little Himalayan mammals
—Pere David's vole and the Sichuan burrowing shrew. Mostly, though, it is
birdlife that abounds here. Tesias, red-headed laughing thrushes, sivas, tree
partridges and tree creepers, the warbler and the green-tailed sunbird.
Winter visitors include sapphire flycatchers and yellow-bellied
flowerpeckers. In the marshy summit area are surprisingly tame pygmy
wren-babblers, woodcocks and rufus-throated tree partridges.

There are bungalows and camping facilities in Doi Inthanon, and
visitors should remember warm clothing for the winter months.

Doi Suthep National Park

This is a fairly new national park. It is within very easy reach of Chiang Mai and can be combined with sightseeing—Doi Suthep's Wat Phrathat and its holy rèlics and the royal summer palace of Buping are the main attractions.

Most large mammals long ago fled this area, but it is still very rich in birdlife. There have been 303 different species of birds recorded here, some of them very rare elsewhere—the wedge-tailed green pigeon, the green and purple cochoas, spot-throated brown jungle babblers, ultramarine flycatchers, among many others. If nature is what interests you, do not depart after seeing the temple and the summer palace, or even after the Meo village nearer the summit. Instead explore some of the interesting walks which are easily followed and suitable for even the faintest heart. One trail begins near the park headquarters to the right of a parking lot on the left side of the road. Further up is a rough track also suitable for walkers. You don't need a guide and, although it takes a while, the walking is easy on both trails.

There are two bungalows in the park, two dormitory residences each accommodating 40, and a campground near the Khonthathan Waterfall.

Khao Yai National Park

This was the first and is still the biggest of Thailand's national parks. It is in the Northeast. In 1971 it was listed among the world's top five parks, and it has recently been named an ASEAN National Heritage Site—so if you can see no other national park in Thailand, you should try to get to this one.

It is 205 kilometres northeast of Bangkok, and it is really best to travel by car, since you can then use it inside the 2,000-kilometre park. However, there are also tour buses daily between Bangkok's northern bus terminal and Nakhon Ratchasima, stopping at Pak Chong where you can then hire a minibus to the park headquarters. Bargain over the fare and try to find others to share the trip.

Khao Yai contains some of the largest remaining areas of rain forest in Asia—extensive evergreen forest, upland marshes, grassland and, of course, wildlife galore. This is one of the rare places in Thailand where large mammals roam free—elephants, tigers, deer and gibbons. There are also Asiatic black bears, leopards, golden cats, mouse deer, barking deer, slow loris and many other species of mammals. There are some 10,000 gibbons, and many visitors report seeing gangs of white-handed gibbons roaming around even the most frequented areas of the park. For those who like them, there is a whole cave full of bats at Luk Chang Mountain, and for bird watchers it is a paradise. Among the many species of birds rare elsewhere but seen here are silver pheasants, pompadour green pigeons, forest eagle owls, brown needletails, the blue pitta, the yellow-footed green pigeon, orioles and wrynecks. There are also four varieties of hornbill to be seen.

There are many trails through the park, long and short, often leading to waterfalls, and for the adventurous there are rope-strung bridges across the torrents which wind through the park, plenty of campsites and picnic places and observation towers from which to look out for wildlife. A special attraction in Khao Yai is known as night-shining. A truck big enough for 40 travels through the park, using a searchlight to light up the wildlife roaming the forest at that time—deer, porcupine, tigers and perhaps even an elephant.

Twelve bungalows are for rent, plus four 20-man tents and six 30-man tents. There is also a campsite, plus a TAT restaurant, tennis court and golf course.

Sam Lan National Park

This is the nearest park to Bangkok, only an hour's drive north. It consists mainly of hills, waterfalls, forest, grass and bamboo groves.

The animal and birdlife is not as rich and varied as in other parks, but that is the price you pay for its convenient siting near Bangkok. Nevertheless, it does have slow loris, wild pigs, mouse deer and porcupines, among other resident small mammals. There are not a lot of birds, but common among those who do live there are francolins, red jungle fowl, shikra, parakeets and flycatchers.

This is Bangkok's green lung, and there are many picnic spots and pleasant walks in peaceful surroundings. Campsites and dormitory accommodation are available.

Tarutao National Park

This is a series of 51 rocky islets off the southwest coast, with headquarters on Tarutao Island. Several of the islands conform to the classic desert isle recipe—long white beaches, unspoilt coral reefs and untouched tropical rain forest. They even, in certain cases, used to boast pirates.

Now they mainly support a few small mammals, a large variety of birdlife and beautiful marine gardens of fish, coral and ocean-dwelling creatures. From September to April sea turtles make the painful trek to lay eggs in the sand, which hatch to face the immense dangers posed by marine predators waiting for these juicy little innocents to hatch.

There is an excellent little museum on Tarutao Island, plus good walking trails, clear seas and marvellous snorkelling and diving. Experts recommend at least three days for this trip, and remember that May to October is the rainy season, which can mean cloudy seas as well as wet.

There is room for 200 guests at the headquarters on Tarutao Island, in simple but attractive bungalows, single rooms and camping grounds. Nearby Adang Island also has facilities for about 80 people.

You can get there in a number of ways. By bus from Hat Yai to Pak Bara, using taxi transfers if necessary, then hiring a boat in Pak Bara for the sea trip to Tarutao. There are no boats on Tarutao for hire so you must either keep your boat, if you want to travel between islands, or at least arrange a return pick-up time. It is not cheap to do this, so try to get together with other people and share the 3,000 baht plus to Tarutao. It will cost more to hold the boat and to travel to the other islands. But it really is a once-in-a-lifetime trip, so don't lose out through penny-pinching.

Tham Than Lot National Park

This is the smallest of the four national parks in beautiful Kanchanaburi province, but it has some caves well worth exploring—one is 300 metres long with a stream flowing through it, another huge as a natural cathedral—several equally spectacular waterfalls and numerous forest trails.

Some of the larger mammals can be seen here—tiger, elephant, Asiatic black bear, gibbons, deer and a great variety of birds.

There are nine bungalows and a restaurant open at weekends. The park is 97 kilometres from Kanchanaburi. You can travel by car or take the bus from Kanchanaburi to Ban Nong Pru, where you can hire a minibus.

General Information

Most of the parks have a purely nominal entrance fee of a few baht, and those areas designated as wildlife sanctuaries and non-hunting areas are completely free.

Take with you a flashlight, raincoat, insect repellent, towel and something to carry water in and drink from.

If the path you wish to walk on does not seem to be well marked, you would be wise to take a guide with you.

If you want to stay in the parks, it is a good idea to book accommodation ahead by writing to:

Reservation Office,
National Parks Division,
Royal Forest Department,
Phahonyothin Road,
Bang Khen, Bangkok.

Be specific about time, the number of your party and so on, and give some alternative dates too. Experts think it is probably wiser to make your reservations in person—Thai officials do not usually rush to reply to their mail.

As a note of general guidance, remember that these parks are meant to be places of conservation. Therefore, do not take away souvenirs in the form of plants, shells, insects or coral. Do not leave unwelcome souvenirs of your visit behind you either—no litter, and no dropped cigarettes to burn down the hillsides. Don't take noisy radios or cassette players in with you, as they are destructive to the very peace and quiet you presumably went to enjoy.

Hotels in Bangkok

Note: As room rates are continually being revised upwards, we have simply classified the hotels into the following categories: Budget (B), Moderate (M), Expensive (E) and Very Expensive (VE).

Airport Hotel (E)
333 Chert Wadthakas Road,
Don Muang, Bangkok 10210
Tel: 5239177/8, 5239322
Cable: APINTERHTL
Telex: TH 87424, 87425 AIRHOTL

Ambassador (E)
Soi 11, Sukhumvit Road
Tel: 2515141, 2510404
Cable: AMTEL
Telex: TH 82910

Asia (M-E)
296 Phya Thai Road
Tel: 2811433, 2820121/9
Cable: ASIAHOTEL
Telex: TH 82722

Atlanta Club (B)
Soi 2, Sukhumvit Road
Tel: 2526068/9

Bangkok Centre (M)
328 Rama IV Road
Tel: 2351780/99
Cable: BACENHO
Telex: TH 72067/8

Bangkok Palace (E)
1091/336 New Phetchaburi Road
Tel: 2525700/5
Cable: BKK PALACE
Telex: TH 84278/9

The Bangkok Peninsula (VE)
155 Rajdamri Ave.
Tel: 2516127
Telex: TH 20004 BKK PENN

Century (B-M)
9 Rajprarob Road
Tel: 2453271/3, 2781596/8
Cable: CENTURYHTL

Continental (B-M)
971/16 Phahonyothin Road
Tel: 2781596/8
Cable: CONNENTAL
Telex: TH 84883

Dusit Thani (VE)
Saladaeng Circle, Rama IV Road
Tel: 2331130
Cable: DUSITOTEL
Telex: TH 81170, 81027

Erawan (E)
494 Rajdamri Road
Tel: 2529100/19
Cable: ERAWAN BANGKOK
Telex: TH 82189

Federal (B)
27 Soi 11, Sukhumvit Road
Tel: 2525143, 2529036
Cable: FEDERHOTEL

First (E)
2 Phetchaburi Road
Tel: 2525010/9
Cable: FIRSTHOTEL
Telex: TH 82027

Florida (M)
43 Phya Thai Road
Tel: 2524141
Cable: FLOHOTEL
Telex: TH 3300

Fortuna (B)
19 Soi 5, Sukhumvit Road
Tel: 2515121/5
Cable: FORTUNAHOTEL

Golden Dragon (M)
20/21 Ngam Wong Wan Road
Tel: 5884414/5
Telex: TH 87667

Golden Horse (M)
5/1-2 Damrongrug Road
Tel: 2817388, 2817593

Grace (B-M)
12 Soi Nana North, Sukhumvit
Road
Tel: 2529170, 2522530
Cable: GRACEHOTEL
Telex: TH 82221

Hilton·International Bangkok (VE)
2 Wireless Road
Tel: 2517111, 2527380
Cable: HILTEL BKK
Telex: TH 72206 HILBKK

Hyatt Central Plaza (E)
1691 Phahonyothin Road,
Bangkhen
Tel: 2701820/35
Telex: 72027 HYATTRC TH,
20173 HYATTBK TH

Impala (M)
9 Soi 24, Sukhumvit Road
Tel: 3913917, 3910038
Cable: IMPAHOTEL
Telex: TH 84056

Indra Regent (E)
Rajprarob Road
Tel: 2511111, 2521111
Cable: INDRAHOTEL
Telex: TH 82723

Liberty (B)
215 Prapipat Road, Sapan Kwai
Tel: 2790606, 2798913/7
Cable: LIBERTOTEL

Majestic (B-M)
97 Ratchadamnoen Ave.
Tel: 2815000, 2815115
Cable: MAJESTIC

Malaysia (B)
54 Soi Ngam Duplee, Rama IV
Road
Tel: 2863582
Cable: MALAYSIA HOTEL

Mandarin (E)
662 Rama IV Road
Tel: 2334980/9
Cable: MANDOTEL
Telex: TH 97689, 84131

Manhattan (E)
Soi 15, Sukhumvit Road
Tel: 2527141/9
Cable: HOTELMAN
Telex: TH 87272

Manohra (E)
412 Suriwong Road
Tel: 2345070
Cable: MANORAOTEL
Telex: TH 82114

Miami (B)
2 Soi 13, Sukhumvit Road
Tel: 2525140/2, 2527379
Cable: MIAMIHOTEL

Miramar (B)
777 Mahachai Road
Tel: 2211711, 2224191/5
Cable: MIRAMAR

Montien (VE)
54 Suriwong Road
Tel: 2337060, 2348060
Cable: MONTEL
Telex: TH 81038, 82938

Morakot (B)

2802 New Phetchaburi Road
Tel: 3140761/3

Narai (E)
222 Silom Road
Tel: 2333350
Cable: NARAIHOTEL
Telex: TH 81175 NARITEL

New Amarin (M)
477 Si Ayutthaya Road
Tel: 2452661/7
Cable: NEWAMRIN
Telex: 82089 NEWARIN TH

New Empire (B)
572 Yawaraj Road
Tel: 2346990/6
Cable: EMPIREGO

New Imperial (VE)
6 Soi Ruam Rudee, Wireless Road
Tel: 2520450/7
Cable: IMPERHOTEL
Telex: TH 82301 IMPER

New Nana (M)
4 Soi 2, Sukhumvit Road
Tel: 2524101, 2501210/9
Cable: NANAHOTEL

New Peninsula (M)
295/3 Suriwong Road
Tel: 2343910/6
Cable: PENHO
Telex: TH 84079 PENINHO

New Trocadero (M)
343 Suriwong Road
Tel: 2348920/9
Cable: TROCADERO
Telex: TH 81061 NEWTROC

Oriental (VE)
48 Oriental Ave.
Tel: 2348621/9
Cable: ORIENHOTEL
Telex: TH 82997

Park (B)
6 Soi 7, Sukhumvit Road
Tel: 2525110/1
Cable: PARK HOTEL

Parliament (B-M)
402 Visutkasat Road
Tel: 2817411, 2817026

President (E)
135/26 Gaysorn Road
Tel: 2529880/9
Cable: PRESIDOTEL
Telex: TH 81194

Prince (B)
1537/1 New Phetchaburi Road
Tel: 2516171/6
Cable: PRINCEHL

Ra-Jah (M-E)
18 Soi 4, Sukhumvit Road
Tel: 2525102/9
Cable: RAJAHOTEL
Telex: TH 87385

R.S. (Rajsubhamitra) (M)
269 Larn Luang Road
Tel: 2813644
Cable: RSHOTEL
Telex: TH 87688 RSHOTEL

Rama Gardens (E-VE)
9/9 Viphavadi Rangsit Road
Tel: 5795400, 5791113
Cable: RAMA GARDEN
Telex: TH 84250

Rama Tower (E)
981 Silom Road
Tel: 2341010/9
Cable: RAMATOW
Telex: TH 82998

Ramada (B)
1169 New Road
Tel: 2348971/5

Reno (B)
Soi Kasemsan I, Rama I Road
Tel: 2526121
Cable: RENOHOTEL

Rex (B-M)
762/1 Sukhumvit Road
Tel: 3910100
Cable: REXHOTEL

Rose (B-M)
118 Suriwong Road
Tel: 2336360/2

Royal (B-M)
2 Ratchadamnoen Ave.
Tel: 2229111/7
Cable: ROYALHOTEL
Telex: TH 7266 EDTRAVEL
CAREROYAL

Royal Orchid (VE)
2 Captain Bush Lane, Siphya Road
Tel: 2345599
Telex: TH 84491 ROYORCH

Sheraton (E)
80 Suriwong Road
Tel: 2335160/74
Cable: SHERATON
Telex: TH 81167 SHERBKK

Siam (M)
1777 New Phetchaburi Road
Tel: 2525081
Cable: SIAM HOTEL

Siam Inter-Continental (VE)
Rama I Road
Tel: 2529040, 2529060
Cable: INHOTELCOR
Telex: TH 81155 SIAMINTR

Thai (B-M)
78 Prachathipatai Road
Tel: 2813633, 2822833
Cable: THAIHOTEL

Victory (M)
322 Silom Road
Tel: 2339060
Cable: VICTORY HOTEL
Telex: TH 81089 VICTORY

Viengtai (M)
42 Tanee Road, Banglampoo
Tel: 2828672/4
Cable: VIENGTAIHOTEL
Telex: TH 82976

White Inn (B)
Soi 4, Sukhumvit Road
Tel: 2527090, 2511662

Windsor (M-E)
8 Soi 20, Sukhumvit Road
Tel: 3915300, 3925294/8
Cable:WINDHOTEL
Telex: TH 82081 WINDHTL

World (B)
1196 New Phetchaburi Road
Tel: 3144340/6

YMCA (B)
27 Sathorn Tai Road
Tel: 2861542, 2862580

YWCA (B)
13 Sathorn Tai Road
Tel: 2861936

Index

A

Adang Island 132
agriculture 11, 62, 71, 94-96, 97, 103
Agriculture Department 17
airport 17
Airport Beach 124
Akha 96, 99-101
amulet market 45
Ancient City 49
Andaman Sea 122
Angkor Wat 72
Ang Sila 63
Anuradhapura 107
Ao Karon 122
Ao Kata 122
Ao Mae Hat 117
ASEAN 11, 16, 128
Asoka, King 57
Ayutthaya 7, 53-55, 63, 118

B

Bali 113
Ban Ang Thong 113
Ban Chiang 73
Ban Doi Pui 91
Ban Don 113
Bangkok 32-49
Bang Pa-In 55
Bang Saen 63-64
Ban Kai 117
Ban Khao 55
Ban Khun Khong 101
Ban Nong Pru 132
Ban Phe 70
beer 30
Big Buddha 115
birds' nests 118
Bo Luang Plateau 103
books 85-87, 115
Bophut 115
Bo Sang (Umbrella Village) 83

boxing, Thai 48, 68, 120
brassware 47
Bridge on the River Kwai 55, 59
bronzeware 22
Buddha's footprint 124
Buddhism 7, 9, 23, 44, 57, 80, 105
Buddhist Lent 14
bull-fighting 120
Buping Rajanivesana 91, 128
Burma 7, 11, 20, 83, 93, 98, 99
buses 18, 33, 77, 128

C

canoeing 61
celadon 85
Chaiya 112
Chakrapong Cave 64
Chakri Dynasty 8
Chan Kasem Palace 54
Chan Ta Then Waterfall 64
Chanthaburi 70
Chao Mae Sam Muk 63
Chao Phraya River 53
Chao Phya Maha Katsuksuk 8
Chao Sam Phraya Museum 54
Chatuchak Park 46
Chawang Beach 114, 115
Chiang Dao 101
Chiang Khan 73
Chiang Mai 17, 19, 22, 48, 76-94, 97,
  98, 99, 101, 104, 105, 126, 128
Chiang Mai National Museum 87
Chiang Rai 80, 91, 92, 94, 97, 98,
  99, 101, 103, 105
Chiang Saen 93-94, 104
Ching Pret 14
Chom Thong 91, 126
Chonburi 62-63
Chong Kai War Cemetery 59
Chulalongkorn, King 8, 14
cinema 48, 115
climate 12
cock-fighting 68
communications 19

Constitution Day 15
copperware 47
Coral Island 68
currency 18
customs 16

D
Damnoen Saduak 46
diving 65, 68, 113, 122, 124, 129
Doi Inthanon National Park 89-91,
  92, 126-127
Doi Lolo 98
Doi Suthep 91, 128
dragon boat races 104
drinks 27, 30
Dvaravati 104, 118

E
eating 25-32, 49, 68-69, 87
economy 11
Elephant Roundup 73-76
Emerald Buddha 39, 44, 105
Erawan Hotel shrine 47
Erawan National Park 59, 61
Erawan Waterfall 61
etiquette 22-25
exports 11

F
Fang 91, 98, 99, 101
festivals 12-15
fishing 11, 62, 70, 103, 115, 117, 119,
  122
floating markets 46
food 25-32, 49, 87, 108
Friendship Highway 72
fruit 30-31, 64, 70

G
gems 20, 70, 93
geography 11
Golden Buddha 42
Golden Triangle 92, 93-94

golf 63, 64, 68, 124, 129
Grand Palace 38

H
handicrafts 20-22, 70, 76, 82-85, 91,
  99, 119, 120, 125
hang-gliding 65
Hardrint Beach 117
Hat Nai Beach 122
Hat Nai Yang National Park 122
Hat Pa Dang 64
Hat Yai 120, 132
Hat Yai Nai Temple 120
health 18, 27
hilltribes 61, 76, 85, 89, 91, 92,
  94-104, 108, 126
Hinayana Buddhism 105
Hin Klom Beach 64
Hin Lad Waterfall 115
hire cars 19
Hmong 97
Hong Kong 68, 77
hospitals 18
Hot 92, 97
H'tin 96, 103, 104
Hua Hin 109
Huai Muang 98

I
Immigration Division 16
Indonesia 59, 112

J
jewellery 20, 70, 83, 91
Jinaraj Buddha 108

K
Kaeng Lawa Cave 60
Kamala Bay 124
Kamphaeng Phet 97, 98
Kampuchea 11, 20, 53
Kanchanaburi 55-62, 103, 132
Kanchanaburi War Cemetery 59

Kao Phang Waterfall 59
Kao-Poon Cave 59
Karen 92, 96, 126
Kathin 14
Khamu 96, 103
Khao Kheo Open Zoo 64
Khao Pansa 14
Khao Phloi Waen 70
Khao Sam Roi Yot National Park
   109
Khao Yai National Park 55, 126,
   128-129
Khok Kloi 125, 126
Khonthathan Waterfall 128
Khun Luang Wilanka 103
Khuntan 89
King's Birthday 15
Kin Kuai Salak 14
Ko Kaeo Phitsadan 70, 124
Ko Kaeo Yai 124
Ko Khrok 68
Ko Lan 68
Ko Lin 68
Ko Maeo 119
Ko Nu 119
Ko Phangan 113, 115-117
Korat 72
Ko Samui 108, 113-118, 119, 122
Ko Sichang 64
Ko Sire 124
Ko Tao 113, 117
Ko Yor 119-120
Kru Pudson 115
Kuang Kud Ku rapids 73

L
lace 85
lacquerware 83
Laem Sing Beach 124
Lahu 96, 98
Lamai Beach 114, 115
Lampang 89, 97, 101, 103, 105
Lamphun 89, 104-105
Laos 7, 11, 73, 94, 97, 98, 99, 103

Lawa 96, 103
Ligor 118
Lisu 96, 101
Loei 72
Lolo 99
Lopburi 55
Loy Krathong 15
Luk Chang Mountain 128

M
Mae Chan 101
Mae Hong Son 92, 93, 97, 98, 101,
   103
Mae Klang Waterfall 92
Mae Klong River 57, 59
Mae Kok River 92, 101
Mae Sae 93, 101
Mae Suai 98, 99, 101
Mae Taeng 92, 101
Mahachulalongkorn Buddhist
   University 44
Mahayana Buddhism 72
Mai Khao Beach 124
Makha Puja 12
malaria 18
Malaysia 11, 15, 59, 109, 120
manners 22-25
Marble Temple 44
Marine Zoological Museum 64
market, floating 46
Market, Thieves 47
Market, Weekend 46
massage parlours 48, 71
Mat Lang 115
media 20
Mekong River 73, 93, 94
Mengrai, King 80
Meo 91, 96, 97-98, 104, 126, 128
Mihn 99
Mon 9, 58, 103, 104, 105
money 18
Mongkut, King 8, 57
monks 23, 112, 115, 117
mosques 119

mosquitoes 18, 112, 114
Mrabri 96, 104
Muslim 9, 11, 23, 108
Musur 98

N
Nai Yang Beach 122
Nakhon Pathom 55-57
Nakhon Ratchasima 72, 128
Nakhon Si Thammarat 118-119
nam pla 70
Nam Tok Khao Krathing 70
Nam Tok Phriu 70
Na Muang Waterfall 115
Nan 97, 99, 103, 104
Narathiwat 109
National Museum 39, 47, 112
national parks 55, 59, 61, 72, 76, 89, 92, 108, 109, 122, 125, 126-133
National Theatre 47
newspapers 20
New Year 12
nielloware 20, 118-119
nightlife 48
Night Market 85
Nong Khai 73
Nong Nooch Village 68
northern food 33

O
Ob Luang Gorge 92
opium 96, 98, 99, 101
orchids 68, 76, 89, 127

P
Pak Bara 132
Pak Chong 128
Pak Thong Chai 72
Palembang 118
parasailing 65
Pasteur Institute 45
Patong Beach 122
Patpong 33, 48 50-1,

Pattaya 17, 64-69
Phang Nga Bay 125, 126
Phayao 97
Phetchabun 97
Phetchaburi 97
Phimai 72
Phi Phi Islands 126
Phitsanulok 108
Phrae 97, 101
Phra Pathom Chedi 56-57
Phra Puttahat Mongkol Buddha 120
Phra Sak Tang Tamani 80
Phra Singha Buddha 82
Phrathat Cave 61
Phraya Nakhon Cave 112
Phuket 108, 109, 122-126
Phu Kradung National Park 72
pizza 49, 69
Ploughing Ceremony 14
post office 19
pottery 22, 73, 83, 85, 118
Pramane Ground 38, 39
Pran Buri 109
prostitution 32, 48, 65

R
railway 18, 62, 77, 89, 113, 120
Rama I 42, 44
Rama III 57
Rama IV 8, 57
Rama V 64, 112
Rama VI 8, 57, 120
Rama VII 8
Ramathibodi, King 7
Ramkamhaeng, King 7
rattanware 47, 64, 85
Rawai Beach 122, 124, 126
Rayong 69-70
reclining Buddha 42, 120, 124
Red Cross 45
restaurants 49, 68-69, 87
rice 11, 99, 103, 104, 118, 122
River Kwai 55, 57-62

Royal Family 23, 63, 91, 109
Royal Palace, Ayutthaya 54
Rubber Research Centre 120

S

Saen Muang Mai, King 82
Sai Yok Waterfall 59, 60, 61
Sam Lan National Park 129
samlor 33, 73, 77
Samui 108, 113-118, 119, 122
Sanam Chan Palace 57
San Kamphaeng 83
Sarasin Bridge 125
Sawankhalok 7
sea gypsies 108, 122, 124
self-drive 19
Shan 85, 92, 98
shells 64, 122, 126, 133
Sherman, Emmanuel 112
shopping 20
Siam Society 48
silk 20, 45, 72, 83
silverware 83, 87, 91, 118-119
Singapore 59, 68
Singora 119
Si Racha 64
smiling 25
Snake Farm 45
snorkelling 65, 68, 113, 122, 124, 129
Songkhla 119-120
Songkran 12
Sri Lanka 7, 20, 80, 105, 107
Sri Suriyothi 54
Srivichai 112, 118
stalactites and stalagmites 59, 60, 125, 126
Sukhothai 7, 14, 15, 42, 97, 104, 105-108, 118
Sumatra 112, 118
Surat Thani 112, 113
Surijavoram, King 72
Surin 73
Surin Beach 124
Susan Hoi 126

Suvarnabhumi 57
Suwankhuha Caves 126

T

tailoring 20
Taiwan 68
Tak 97, 98
Tak Sin, King 8, 44
Takua Thung 126
Talay Sap 119
taxi 17, 33
television 20
temple rubbings 42
temples 32, 38-45, 53-54, 57, 72-73, 80-82, 104, 107, 112, 115, 117, 119
Temple of the Dawn 15, 42
tennis 129
Tha Chin Canal 124
Thai boxing 48, 68, 120
Thai dancing 47, 68, 87, 118
Thai food 25-32, 49, 64, 69, 85, 87
Thalang 124, 125
Tham Than Lot National Park 132
Thaton 92
Theravada Buddhism 7, 9, 105
Thieves Market 47
Thompson, Jim 45
Tibet 94, 98, 99
Tiloka, King 82
Tilokorat, King 80
timber 11
tin 11
tipping 18
Ton Nga Chang Waterfall 120
Ton Sai Waterfall National Park 125
Tourism Authority of Thailand 17, 19, 59, 73, 109, 129
traditional medicine 42, 44
transport 18, 33
Trat 62, 70
trekking 61, 76, 89, 91, 92, 112, 117, 126-133
tribal clothing 85, 97-103

Tribal Museum 87
Tribal Research Centre 87, 89, 92
Turatao National Park 129
Turtle Island 117
turtles 124, 129

U
Udon Thani 73
umbrellas 83
Umpai 103

V
Viang Ping Bazaar 85
Vientiane 73
Vietnam 97, 99
Vietnamese 9
Viharn Luang 118
Visakha Puja 4
visas 15

W
Wai Sai Floating Market 46
Wat Arun 15, 42, *130-1*
Wat Benchamabophit 44
Wat Bodhi 117
Wat Cham Thewi 104
Wat Chang Yuen 82
Wat Chedi Luang 82
Wat Chedi Sung 107
Wat Chet Yot 80
Wat Chiang Man 80
Wat Duang Di 82
water scooters 65
water-skiing 65
Wat Intharam 63
Wat Keo 112
Wat Klang 119
Wat Ku Kut 104
Wat Ku Tao 82
Wat Long 112
Wat Mahathat 44
Wat Mahathat, Nakhon Si
  Thammarat 118

Wat Mahathat, Sukhothai 107
Wat Na Phra Lan 115
Wat Na Phra Mane 54
Wat Pa Pao 82
Wat Phailom 44
Wat Phra Boromathat 112
Wat Phra Doi Suthep 91
Wat Phra Kaeo 38
Wat Phra Kaeo, Lampang 105
Wat Phra Maha That 54
Wat Phra Meru 57
Wat Phra Pai Luang 107
Wat Phra Pathom 57
Wat Phra Si Ratana 108
Wat Phra Si Sanphet 53
Wat Phra Singh Luang 82
Wat Phrathat 128
Wat Phra That Haripunchai 104
Wat Phra That Lampang Luang
  105
Wat Phra Thong 124
Wat Phumin 104
Wat Po 42
Wat Rajanadda 45
Wat Rajburana 54
Wat Ratanaram 112
Wat Saket 45
Wat Si Chum 107
Wat Si Sawai 107
Wat Sra Si 107
Wat Suan Dok 80
Wat Suan Mok 112
Wat Tamkhong Paen 73
Wat Thammik Raj 54
Wat Traimit 42
Wat Trapang Thong Lang 107
Wat Yak 119
Weekend Market 46
whisky 30
White Elephant Gate 82
wickerwork 22
wildlife 61, 64, 72, 77, 91, 108, 109,
  112, 126-133

wind-surfing 65
wood-carving 22, 83

Y
Yang 96
Yao 92, 96, 99
Yor 119-120
Yumbri 104